T0194647

Battle Scars *to* Beauty Marks

*18 Week Bible Study on Dealing with Life's
Scars and Making them Beautiful*

Missy Armstrong

WESTBOW
P R E S S®
A DIVISION OF THOMAS NELSON
& ZONDERVAN

WestBow Press books may be ordered through booksellers or by contacting:

WestBow Press
A Division of Thomas Nelson & Zondervan
1663 Liberty Drive
Bloomington, IN 47403
www.westbowpress.com
1 (866) 928-1240

THE HOLY BIBLE, NEW INTERNATIONAL VERSION®,
NIV® Copyright © 1973, 1978, 1984, 2011 by Biblica, Inc.®
Used by permission. All rights reserved worldwide.

Scripture taken from the King James Version of the Bible

ISBN: 978-1-9736-6628-8 (sc)
ISBN: 978-1-9736-6627-1 (e)

Print information available on the last page.

WestBow Press rev. date: 06/24/2019

2 Corinthians 12:9
"But he said to me, "My grace is sufficient for you, for my power is made perfect in weakness." Therefore I will boast all the more gladly about my weaknesses, so that Christ's power may rest on me."

Contents

Chapter 1 - What is a Battle Scar?

"You can't do this!"
    "You are not smart enough."
    "No one will ever read this."
    "Everyone will know the bad decisions you made."
    "They will know you have sinned."
    These are the words running through the back of my head as I started to write this Bible Study. These thoughts I know are from Satan because he has played on my low self-esteem scar for years. All I have to say is but God. But God can give me the words to say. But God made me who I am. But God will use these words to His glory. BUT GOD!!
    I made bad choices that lead to bad situations. I have sinned big time. But God said in 1 John 1:9 "If we confess our sins, he is faithful and just and will forgive us our sins and purify us from all unrighteousness." So HA Satan take that! Over time, I discovered that while God had forgiven me, I had not forgiven myself. And the scars left from my sin and Satan's attacks have left me full of shame and regret. Then a few years ago while putting together a Bible study for a women's group at our church. I came across this verse. I had read it before but this time it just set off in my brain like a fourth of July fireworks show. And for months I kept going back to this verse and pondering it. I had no idea the scale of a journey this verse

was going to take me on. The verse is 2 Corinthians 12:9 "But he said to me, "My grace is sufficient for you, for my power is made perfect in weakness." Therefore I will boast all the more gladly about my weaknesses, so that Christ's power may rest on me." I began to pray, "How do I boast about weaknesses?" And God lead me on an adventure that showed me how to be all right with my scars and boast about my weaknesses.

Here is the thing. I was raised in a Christian home. My parents were youth directors and my grandfather was a preacher. I was raised in a time when you didn't talk about your sin. You put on a dress and went to church and tried to act as normal as possible. That's harder for some than others. I can do a lot of things, but normal is not one. So telling people about things I had done or had been through was just alien to me. Everything inside me was fighting against the idea. However, it ended up being the best fight of my life. Because through this fight I saw how God's hand and power were with me through it all. This book/Bible study is the journey I took with God to make my battle scars beauty marks.

My sister and I are four years apart. We have the same mother and father, grew up in the same town, went to the same schools, attended the same church and even participated in basically the same activities, but we have completely different personalities and completely different scars. She always looks like a million dollars and is well put together. Me... Well I usually look like Jack Nicholson from the shining and my idea of dressing up is wearing my flip-flops with the rhinestones. And I am OK with that. Because God is infinite in His knowledge, and He knows exactly why we are who we are. Even though we are completely different like two sides to the same coin, God can heal us from our scars with the same methods. And I believe he can and will heal you.

Everyone has different scars. Some of us may share some scars. None of us have all the same scars. The Merriam-Webster's Dictionary defines battle scars as a lasting mark from a wound suffered in battle. Scars are a lasting reminder of a wound. Constant nagging of something you did, was done to you, or a situation that happened. Normally, these are not happy things because wounds hurt. Life is a battle and our enemy isn't each other it's Satan.

Ephesians 6:12

> "For our struggle is not against flesh and blood, but against the rulers, against the authorities, against the powers of this dark world and against the spiritual forces of evil in the heavenly realms."

Have you ever noticed that when you are trying to live for God and do what's right; things get hard? Every day is a battle sometimes we come out unscathed, other times we are left with wounds that take days, weeks, months, or even years to heal. If you don't have to fight temptations or situations Satan has thrown at you on a daily basis. You may need to check and see whose side you're fighting on.

We think of scars as unsightly things that we try to cover up and hide. "If we were strong enough, we could have done something else and not been wounded." This is what Satan wants us to think. "A stronger Christian woman would not have made that mistake." That is just Satan trying to break you down and make you feel useless. We can't compare ourselves to others. Comparison only leads to discontent. This is exactly what Satan wants. He wants us beat down, so we do not think we are good enough to serve God. Remember Romans 3: 23 "for all have sinned and fall short of the glory of God." Now after going through this journey with God, every time Satan comes at me with comparisons, I can see what he is doing and turn it back to what God's done for me. Through my weaknesses, God shines through me more. Through this Bible Study, you will see how God power rested on me and how it can rest on you.

There are different types of battle scars. Some scars are physical. I had an emergency C Section when my son was born. So I have a pretty nasty scar running down my belly. These scars may be harder to hide than others. Physical scars are only a fraction of the scars most of us carry. Some scars are emotional. These scars elicit powerful emotions in us. The death of a loved one may be an emotional scar that causes sadness or mourning. Being bullied or abused my lead to emotions of anger and discontent. Mental scars are wounds that create thoughts in your head. These thoughts produced by wounds can be; low self-esteem, anxiety, and fear. Mental scars can take hold of you and paralyze you, keeping you from becoming who God meant to you to be because you don't think you can. The last type of scar is spiritual. This is the most dangerous scar because it is damaging to your relationship with Christ. Spiritual scars are caused by un-confessed sin in our lives or by situations we blame God for. These scars keep you from living your life for Christ. Because you have put up barriers, spiritual walls, between you and God.

What is the difference in a scar and a beauty mark? A beauty mark can be defined as a small natural or artificial mark, considered to enhance someone's attractiveness. We know that a battle scar is a lasting mark from a wound suffered in battle. So why can't a scar be a beauty mark? Margaret Wolfe wrote, "Beauty is in the eye of the beholder." Are we not boasting about our weakness and sharing our scars because we are looking at them the wrong way.

Ecclesiastes 3:11

"He has made everything beautiful in its time. He has also set eternity in the human heart, yet no one can fathom what God has done from beginning to end."

Our scars are reminders of our weaknesses so to us they are ugly. We spend so much time making ourselves more presentable, hiding scars and trying to be as attractive as possible. If we took a portion of that time and worked on our Christian walk, we could see that those scars are also evidence of God's love, power, and grace in you. Your beauty marks are a love letter from God to you.

Dig Deeper:

Take a moment and think about your life.

Pray for God to show to you your scars and weaknesses. Be honest with yourself.

Write down your scars that still hurt and need to be healed.

_____

_____

_____

_____

_____

Read aloud,

> 2 Corinthians 12:9
>
> "But he said to me, "My grace is sufficient for you, for my power is made perfect in weakness." Therefore I will boast all the more gladly about my weaknesses, so that Christ's power may rest on me."

Shout this!

> "My grace is sufficient for you, for my power is made perfect in weakness."

Stop and think about 1 John 1:9

> "If we confess our sins, he is faithful and just
> and will forgive us our sins and purify us from
> all unrighteousness."

Go to God in prayer and confess your sins. List them one by one. And ask God to convict you of any sin you have overlooked.

God is faithful and just to forgive your sin. Now ask God to help you forgive yourself. You were weak and made a mistake. None is perfect except for Jesus Christ. Start moving forward and do your best not to do that sin again.

I challenge you, as you go through your week, take time every day to read 2 Corinthians 12:9 and 1 John 1:9.

Pray every day that God would prepare your heart and mind for this Bible study and the journey you are about to embark on.

Chapter 2 - Transparent Me

Throughout this Bible study; you will see me. You will see the wretched fleshy parts of me. You will see the sin I have had and still have. I am going to be transparent. Because for you to understand how a battle scar can become a beauty mark you have to see how God has healed and worked on me. By being honest, you can see how God changes lives, and you can help others by allowing those battle scars to heal and sharing them with others.

This is a list of some of my own battle scars. (This is me)

>   Lost a parent when I was 7
>   Battled addiction
>   Loved someone with cancer
>   Had a miscarriage
>   Raised a child with special needs
>   Had a problem with gossiping and been on gossiped about
>   Took care of someone with Alzheimer's
>   Battled low self-esteem
>   Got pregnant before I was married
>   Is Lazy
>   Is prideful
>   Can be jealous

» Does not pray and read the Bible as much as I should
» Is not patient
» Spent years out of God's will because I was selfish.
» Been in an abusive relationship.

I could go on, but that book would be too big to carry around. I battle every day with my own flesh, and I am sure that many of you do too. Everything listed above has caused me scars and pain. But the thing is God is bigger than all those things. And many of them I brought on myself because I refused to follow God completely. My fleshly desires overpowered my desire to serve God. I told you at times I can be a wretched fleshly beast. I am broken and bruised and the only thing that holds this mess people call "Missy" together is God's Love and strength.

Isaiah 41:10 says, "So do not fear, for I am with you; do not be dismayed, for I am your God. I will strengthen you and help you; I will uphold you with my righteous right hand." Hallelujah! I need God to hold me together. Missy tried doing it for herself and that is now referred to as "The Dark Years." God has plans for us, but He has also given us free will. So we make mistakes. We mess up, and we end up scars.

I like to think of God's permissive plan like a GPS. We know that life is a journey. We get in the car and type in our destination. For Christians, once we are saved; we pray and read the Bible and head out down God's road. If the GPS tells us to turn right, and we turn left, it recalculates and finds another suitable route or asked you to do a u-turn. So when God tells us to turn right, and we run left he recalculates. If we continue to ignore what the GPS tells us, it will continue to try to find a new route. You may end up on a dirt road in a sketchy neighborhood. God allows us to make wrong turns and end up places we never intended while He is always trying to direct us back to the main highway. For example, Jonah, God said zig and Jonah zagged. You can read through the story in the book of Jonah in the Old Testament. I suggest you do. But for this study, I am just going to do a little recap for you.

God asked Jonah to go Nineveh and tell the people there to stop sinning and turn to God. Jonah didn't want to help those people. He knew they were evil, and he wanted them punished for their sins. So Jonah ran and jumped on a ship going the other direction. A storm came up and the people on the boat knew they were going down. The sailors decided that the storm was Jonah's fault. He must have done something wrong to make his god so angry. So they asked Jonah, "What have you done? What God do you believe in? What can we do to make this storm stop?"

Jonah told them, "I believe in the Lord, the God of heaven, who made the sea and the land, and I am running away from something God asked me to do. It is my fault this is happening. If you throw me into the sea, the storm will stop." Then the captain and the crew looked out to sea as a huge fish came and swallowed up Jonah. Jonah stayed in the fish for three days and three nights. After the third day, God told the fish to spit Jonah out onto dry land. And the fish did just that.

To be honest, Jonah zagged pretty hard. God recalculated and directed Jonah back to the right path. Some of my scars come from my own zagging and repeated left turns when God is telling me to go right. If I am honest, more than once I have found myself metaphorically in the middle of nowhere on a dirt road wondering if that rickety old wooden bridge can even hold me up. Spoiler alert! It didn't and I fell into the muddy rock bottom of life. God was telling me over and over, "turn, turn,

turn." But, I gave in to selfish flesh and landed in places God didn't intend for me.

Here is the beauty of it. I messed it up, I ran away, and I sinned. But God forgave me, gave me grace and now can use that for his glory. By that I mean, others can see God's love, mercy, and grace through my life even though I spent years letting Satan tempt me into sin. Satan didn't make me sin, I did that. That is the first step to seeing your battle scars as beauty marks, being honest yourself and God. No one made you sin.

Some of my scars have nothing to do sin they are just life. Deaths of people I loved. Watching people suffer when I couldn't fix it and scars caused by other peoples sins. When my grandfather had Alzheimer's, I lived with him for a while. That time with him I cherish however it hurt so bad to watch him deteriorating as he did. Many times, I caught myself just crying and questioning why this was happening. This happened during the dark years and even a few years after my grandfather's death I was still angry and wallowing in self-pity. Because oh poor me, this thing happened. After coming back to God, He led me to James 2: 2-8. It is amazing how the Bible was there all the time, but I was too wretched, fleshy and selfish to pick it up.

James 1:2-8 reads, Consider it pure joy, my brothers and sisters, whenever you face trials of many kinds because you know that the testing of your faith produces perseverance. Let perseverance finish its work so that you may be mature and complete, not lacking anything. If any of you lacks wisdom, you should ask God, who gives generously to all without finding fault, and it will be given to you. But when you ask, you must believe and not doubt, because the one who doubts is like a wave of the sea, blown and tossed by the wind. That person should not expect to receive anything from the Lord. Such a person is double-minded and unstable in all they do.

Alzheimer's tested my faith and after the dark years when I had confessed my sins and came back to God he did strengthen me. This allowed me to empathize with others in the same situation and even strengthened my faith for raising a son with autism. These scars that hurt and cut deep can heal and will heal if you allow God to do His work in and on you.

1 Peter 5:10 says, "And the God of all grace, who called you to his eternal glory in Christ, after you have suffered a little while, will himself restore you and make you strong, firm and steadfast." If your scars are like these, there is hope; the hope of eternity with those who have passed away and were saved. Hope that God will restore you; hope that will He make you firm and steadfast. God is hope and the suffering is only for a little while.

Dig Deeper

I hope at the end of the last chapter you prayed for God to show you your scars.

Take a moment and look at the list you made in the last chapter.

Since you have prayed has God brought anymore to mind? If so, list them here.

_____

_____.

_____

_____

Think about the times God has had to recalculate in your life.

Read aloud,

> 1 Peter 5:10- "And the God of all grace, who called you to his eternal glory in Christ, after you have suffered a little while, will himself restore you and make you strong, firm and steadfast."

Pray and ask God to redirect you on to the path He wants you on.

If you feel separated from God or if you are running from God take time this week each day and read the prayer of Jonah in Jonah 2:

"From inside the fish Jonah prayed to the Lord his God. ² He said:
"In my distress I called to the Lord,
    and he answered me.
    From deep in the realm of the dead I called for help,
    and you listened to my cry.
³ You hurled me into the depths,
    into the very heart of the seas,
    and the currents swirled about me;
    all your waves and breakers
    swept over me.
⁴ I said, 'I have been banished
    from your sight;
    yet I will look again
    toward your holy temple.'
⁵ The engulfing waters threatened me,
    the deep surrounded me;
    seaweed was wrapped around my head.
⁶ To the roots of the mountains I sank down;
    the earth beneath barred me in forever.
    But you, Lord my God,
    brought my life up from the pit.
⁷ "When my life was ebbing away,
    I remembered you, Lord,
    and my prayer rose to you,
    to your holy temple.
⁸ "Those who cling to worthless idols
    turn away from God's love for them.
⁹ But I, with shouts of grateful praise,
    will sacrifice to you.
    What I have vowed I will make good.
    I will say, 'Salvation comes from the Lord.'"

[10] And the LORD commanded the fish, and it vomited Jonah onto dry land."

If you don't feel separated from God but you are wounded and feel that you have suffered or are suffering, read 1 Peter 5:10 every day.

> 1 Peter 5:10- "And the God of all grace, who called you to his eternal glory in Christ, after you have suffered a little while, will himself restore you and make you strong, firm and steadfast."

Continue to pray daily to God to work in and through you.

Chapter 3- Go to the Doctor

The first thing we do when we get seriously hurt or sick is to go to the doctor. So why is it so hard for us when we are wounded in a non-physical way to take it to God? He is the Great Physician. As a woman, I am guilty of trying to fix it first, especially as a mom, because I'm the mom that's my job, to make things better. God says in Philippians 4:6-7 "Do not be anxious about anything, but in every situation, by prayer and petition, with thanksgiving, present your requests to God. And the peace of God, which transcends all understanding, will guard your hearts and your minds in Christ Jesus." I know this verse and I hold on to it. But still, it is hard for me to relinquish control.

For the transformation of a battle scar to begin; you have to give God control. When you go to the doctor, you try your best to tell the doctor all your symptoms. We list them like a grocery list. For some reason, when we pray make blanket statements. "God forgive me of my sins." "Help my family." "Heal my scars." It's as if we think God can't be bothered with little old me. Imagine telling your doctor or spouse, "Help me feel better." the first thing they would say is, "What exactly is the problem?" God is all-knowing. But He wants to have a relationship with you. He doesn't just want to take your order. This is our greatest weapon against Satan. We can use it to talk to and hear from God. It strengthens your relationship with God.

Think of it like this. If you had a spouse or best friend that only talked to you once a day. When they talked to you they came in gave you a vague compliment and started listing things they wanted. Before you could say anything they said whatever you want to do and walked out. Then every day came back and did the same things. That would not be a strong relationship. How close would you and your spouse or boyfriend or best friend be if every time you spoke someone else was right there with you. You go to the movies or out to eat and there is this other person. Driving in the car there is always someone in the back seat. The relationship is never going to get to a point of complete trust or intimacy because someone is always there. When we only pray in church, bible study or with family, this happens with God we can't get more intimate with him because of our surroundings.

When Jesus prayer he often went out on his own, and he never just listed his wants. Frequently in our busy lives, we treat prayer like a drive-through window. God deserves so much more from us than a list of all the things we need help with. God is so patient with us, and he listens even we when have stopped listening to him. Prayer should be a conversation, not a speech. After prayer, we shouldn't just walk away. We need to sit in silence for a minute pondering what we said. Waiting for God to speak to us.

I have had so many Christians say to me, "God doesn't speak to Me." or "God doesn't talk to us like he did in the Bible." My answer is always, "Oh, yes He does! People are just not listening to what He has to say." Have you ever said or thought those things? "God doesn't speak to me." or "God doesn't talk to us like he did in the Bible." Can you honestly say that when you said or thought that you were sitting and letting God speak to you? You may not get a burning much like Moses but you will hear a still small voice that came to Elijah.

In the past, I have struggled with prayer. Mainly because, I didn't want to waste God's time with my tiny problems. So I prayed "God, teach me to Pray." God answered with "I already have, you know what to do." So I went back to the Bible to the Lord's Prayer and saw it in a brand-new light. I began talking about prayer to others and My Papaw, the preacher, said something that has always stuck with me. He said, "People ask things in prayer, but they ask for the wrong reasons."

James 4: 2-3 says "You desire but do not have, so you kill. You covet but you cannot get what you want, so you quarrel and fight. You do not have because you do not ask God. [3] When you ask, you do not receive, because you ask with wrong motives, that you may spend what you get on your pleasures." He went on to explain that we need to understand why we want someone healed. The answer is: they can have more time to serve God and be a witness. It's the same with any request a new job, a car, a baby anything. We should ask for it and tell God why we need it. And the "Why" should always be to further God's Kingdom.

In Matthew 6: 5-15, Jesus taught us how to pray in the Lord's Prayer. This is a template on how our prayers should be structured or what we should include in our prayers.

Our Father, who art in heaven- Address God and think about coming to Him. Really picture it in your mind. You are entering God's throne room and kneeling at His feet. What a humbling feeling it is. Knowing that you are not worthy, but He loves you just the same. When you get into this mindset, the next step is easy.

Hallowed be Thy Name- Praise God for who He is. Just let the praises flow. Be authentic. If you feel a song, sing it. If a verse comes to mind, say it. Take a moment and just bring praise to God. My husband loves the saying, "What if you woke up tomorrow with only what you thanked God for today." take a moment here and just praise God with thanksgiving.

Thy kingdom come, thy will be done, on earth as it is in heaven.- Let him know that you are a servant of His will and that you will follow his commands. Honestly tell Him your desire is to see his will done. To see His word shared and people saved.

Give us this day our daily bread. - Ask for the things you need or make requests. Now is where you get specific about what you need. I need you to help me be honest and admit I messed up. Please heal my wounds etc. Make heartfelt and be humble about your requests.

And forgive us our trespasses, - Confess your sins and ask for forgiveness. Make a list if you need to but be specific here as well. When you recognize the sins you have committed it is much easier to try to repent and turn away from them. You can also ask God to convict you of sins that you overlooked, to help you grow closer to Him.

<u>As we forgive those who trespass against us.</u> - Ask prayer for your enemies or those who hurt you. Jesus was very adamant about loving your enemies and praying for those who mistreat you. If you are struggling to forgive someone for their actions, start praying for that person daily. God will open your heart and before you know it you will have forgiven that person and you will be praying for God to bless them.

<u>And lead us not into temptation, but deliver us from evil.</u> - Ask for help and deliverance from Satan's temptations. I used to go to church with a man who would always pray for God to "Put a hedge of protection around each of us." I would visualize this as a big hedge like in the old English or French gardens. Those big hedge mazes that are taller than you and so thick nothing is getting through. Ask for that hedge or that impenetrable wall to protect you daily.

<u>For thine is the kingdom, and the power, and the glory, forever and ever.</u> - Praise God again and submit to His will for you. My husband likes to call this the praise sandwich. Start with praise and the confession, forgiveness, the request, and end praise. Never forget that God deserves so much more praise than we can give.

<u>Amen.</u> - Amen means "So be it." You end your prayer with your will is greater than mine. I will follow your way. Your will be done. Closing in Jesus' Name. Because it's His blood that

allowed you to have the honor of speaking to God directly.

As you pray remember to be specific in your needs, recite scripture to remind God of His promises, and cry out to God or pray with everything you have in you. Giving all you have to Him will result in peace, understanding and a desire to be closer to him. The more time we take in prayer and conversation with God the stronger our relationship is with Him. This leads to a much more joyful, abundant and spirit-filled life than you have ever known.

My brain is running all the time. Trying to block out everything and pray was a battle for me. I would get halfway into a prayer and my mind would start thinking about what I was cooking for supper or what we needed to do or what we needed to pick up. One thing I started doing was to make a list. I didn't write out the prayer. Just the order and I would make a list of requests, a list of praises, and then make a list of sins, to ask forgiveness for. It helped me stay on track and when something moved off my request list I could put in the praise list. It also helped me target sin in my life and actively try to get it out or avoid it.

Coloring while I pray has also helped keep my mind focused on the task. A few years ago, I was given a journaling Bible. With pictures ready to color. I love to get that out with my lists and color as I pray. You may not need lists or colors, but if you do find that your mind wonders you can try things like this to help you stay focused. There is a lady I know that crochets while she prays. Find things that distract you and take them away as you pray. Find things that help you stay in that moment with God and use those to assist you. Remember to sit in silence for a while after your prayer.

Dig Deeper

Reread James 4: 2-3

> "You desire but do not have, so you kill. You covet but you cannot get what you want, so you quarrel and fight. You do not have because you do not ask God. When you ask, you do not receive, because you ask with wrong motives, that you may spend what you get on your pleasures."

Have you asked for things with the wrong motives?

_____

_____

Read James 1: 6

> "But when you ask, you must believe and not doubt, because the one who doubts is like a wave of the sea, blown and tossed by the wind."

Have you asked for things with doubt in your heart?

_____

_____

_____

_____

What ways can you improve your prayer life? (Ex. Fewer distractions, praising more, praying for those who hurt me, etc.)

_____

_____

_____

_____

Take a moment right now to go to God's throne room and praise him. Ask for nothing just have a thanksgiving praise prayer.

Take at least 10 minutes a day for the next week to sit down with God in prayer.

Make lists or start a prayer journal to help you, not only stay focused but to see how God is working.

Don't forget the moments of silence to listen for God.

Read Philippians 4:6-7 daily.
Philippians 4:6-7

> "Do not be anxious about anything, but in every situation, by prayer and petition, with thanksgiving, present your requests to God. [7] And the peace of God, which transcends all understanding, will guard your hearts and your minds in Christ Jesus."

Chapter 4- Get Your Prescription

I had to go to the doctor recently because I received an injury doing a play at our community theater. In a scene with my sister, we wrestled over an exercise ball. I think she may have hurt me on purpose. No, I'm just joking. I don't think she really did it on purpose, although our sibling rivalry is epic. Sometimes we do allow our wretched fleshy selves out. But we always love and support each other. Well back to the story. I had swelling around my ribs that was quite painful. The doctor examined me and did an x-ray. Then she gave me instructions, told me not to work that area and gave me a prescription for anti-inflammatory pills. I left went to the pharmacy, picked up the medications and followed the doctor's orders.

It was easy to do what the doctor told me to do. I trusted that it would make me feel better. Then I thought why do we not follow God's prescription? We have it right there in his word. We say we trust God, but again our fleshy self is telling us you don't need to do that. Women and teens are often saying to me, "I don't know what God wants me to do." The first thing I say is, "Have you asked Him? And have you studied the Bible?" People say it doesn't say, "Missy, get up on Monday morning and start writing a bible study." No, it doesn't but it does tell me to listen to when God speaks. It does say that the Holy Spirit will direct us. And it says to use the gifts God has given you to serve others.

So you prayed and studied the Bible, but you still hurt. You still have scars. You still lack direction. It's true that sometimes God may answer prayer with not now or wait. So what do we do in the meantime? A few years back I did a study on Nehemiah. I loved it and learned so much. I suggest it to anyone. If you have never studied Nehemiah, I would say you are missing out on a huge learning opportunity. In Nehemiah, they want to rebuild Jerusalem. One of the things that has stuck with me is in Nehemiah 2: 18 (KJV) which says, "Then I told them of the hand of my God which was good upon me; as also the king's words that he had spoken unto me. And they said, Let us rise up and build. So they strengthened their hands for this good work." They strengthened their hands for this good work. They got themselves ready to do the job that God had given them. So when God has moved you into the waiting room, don't just stand around waiting for your name to be called. Be productive. Strengthen your hands, through Bible study and doing what the bible tells you. Or like I said in Chapter 2, follow god's GPS and get back on the right path.

The Bible tells you exactly what God wants and how to live. So while you are parked in the waiting room, pick up the Bible and start studying. When the Holy Spirit convicts you, make a point to follow His lead. For example, If you are studying Matthew and you are convicted about feeding the hungry or taking care of the poor or widows. You know what God says to do. So do it. Or if you love to gossip and the Holy Spirit keeps leading you to verses about your tongue. Start working on controlling it. If you have sin in your life, start working on getting that sin out.

Bible study is a vital part of a Christian's life. Someone once said an acronym for the Bible was "Basic Instructions Before Leaving Earth." Many times we want to use the Bible as a book of quotes that make you feel better about your situation. The Bible even tells you what it is and how to use it in 2 Timothy 3:16-17 "All Scripture is God-breathed and is useful for teaching, rebuking, correcting and training in righteousness, so that the servant of God may be thoroughly equipped for every good work." Again getting ready or equipped for good work.

Bible study through your local church is a fabulous way to get into the bible and study with the help and input of others. Groups designed for women or people of a certain age and Sunday school are all great ways to get into the word of God. This can help you grow and understand as well as ask questions and get help. However, Bible study should not only exist at church or in a group. Private Bible study fills your soul in ways that are just for you.

Quiet time is a time you set aside every day for prayer and bible study. Imagine I make the best monkey bread in the world. And you came over on Wednesday and ate all you could stand and then didn't eat anything else until the next Wednesday. By Monday, you would be starving. Or even if you came back and ate till you were stuffed on Sunday. How would you be feeling on Tuesday evening or Saturday night? That is how your soul feels when you don't pray or read the Bible but once a week. When we as Christians go to camps, retreats or seminars, we come back filled and excited. Often that tappers of once we return because we are not feeding the soul regularly.

Quiet time should be a time set aside when you can be alone. Jesus prayed alone. (Mark 1:35)

To set up and start a quiet time there are a few things you need to do.

Quiet time-

» Start with a 10 to 15 minute block of time
» In the morning if possible
» Set up a specific place
» Have a Bible, a notebook and Pen
» No interruptions, no phones, no games, and no people!

When my son was in 6th grade it became apparent that he would not be able to stay in public school. He has Asperser's Syndrome, which is on the autism spectrum. With this and a few emotional problems, he was having a terrible time in the school system. My husband and I prayed and God opened doors to allow him to be home schooled for four years. This was great for my boy, but was a pile of work for me. We took time every morning to do a bible study. Everything was overwhelming and started to skip my quiet time to get the school-day ready. I started really feeling a difference. Thinking that the bible study with him was enough had cheapened my own quiet time and it wasn't enough. I had to start waking up 30 minutes earlier and having my time then. Oh! What a difference it made. It was like a weight was lifting off me. If I missed the morning time because some days were tougher than others, I would tell my husband as soon as he came in from work, "I need 30 minutes, take our son on a walk or something." Setting aside a specific time is critical to keeping the habit.

Keeping a notebook is another great way to keep track of what you learned and what God has said to you. You should keep a record of your daily studies. Get a notebook to write down each day's devotion. Study a chapter or paragraph in the Bible. Read it over slowly several times. Ask yourself the following questions:

Does this teach me about sins I need to give up?

_____

_____

_____

_____

Are there promises to claim?

_____

_____

_____

_____

Are there examples to follow?

_____

_____

_____

_____

Are there warnings to consider?

_____

_____

_____

_____

What does it teach me about the Father, Son, and Holy Spirit?

_____

_____

_____

_____

Are there any other truths?

_____

_____

_____

_____

What should I do about these things?

_____

_____

_____

_____

Write down your thoughts. This notebook with help you keep your progress and faithfulness. It will also help you discipline your study and help you reinforce what you have learned. Write down prayer requests and praises in the notebook as well.

_____

_____

_____

_____

_____

_____

_____

Dig Deeper

Do you have a quiet time already? If so, where is it and what time is it.

_____

_____

If not, decide now to set one up.

Time:

Location:

What to study first?

Remember God has given you a prescription. It's up to you to follow the instructions.

Don't be overwhelmed by starting a Bible study. Billy Graham once told a new believer to start in The Gospel of John. Starting your study with one of the Gospels can help even the most spiritually mature Christian be reminded of all Jesus did and all he taught us. Start in one of the Gospels if you do not already have a study set up.

Each day next week take a chapter or paragraph in one of the Gospels. Read it over slowly several times. Ask yourself the following questions:

Does this teach me about sins I need to give up?

_____

_____

_____

_____

Are there promises to claim?

_____

_____

_____

_____

Are there examples to follow?

_____

_____

_____

_____

Are there warnings to consider?

_____

_____

_____

_____

What does it teach me about the Father, Son, and Holy Spirit?

_____

_____

_____

_____

Are there any other truths?

_____

_____

_____

_____

What should I do about these things?

_____

_____

_____

_____

Remember 2 Timothy 3:16-17 "All Scripture is God-breathed and is useful for teaching, rebuking, correcting and training in righteousness, so that the servant of God may be thoroughly equipped for every good work."

Always remember to start and end your quiet time in prayer. Pray now for God to help you stay devoted to Bible study and prayer. Ask Him to help direct your study to help you become the Christian He wants you to be.

Chapter 5- Meditate on the Prescription

When I cook, I love to marinate the meat. Whether it is chicken, pork, beef or venison, something special happens when the meat sits in the juices and spices. It soaks it all up and you can taste it in every bite. For those non-cookers out there, a marinade is a blend of spices and oils or sauces that you put the food in and let it sit. Normally, the longer the food is left to marinate, the more flavorsome it will become. So when I speak to people about meditation, I often tell people to marinate in the word. Sit in it for a while just letting pour over you and soak it up.

Joshua 1:8 says, "Keep this Book of the Law always on your lips; meditate on it day and night, so that you may be careful to do everything written in it. Then you will be prosperous and successful." Meditate day and night. Not read it once and never think about it again. No, meditate day and night. Think about it reread it. Talk about it day and night. Psalms 2:1 reiterates this point.

When I say meditate, I mean Biblical Meditation. I want to be completely clear with you. Biblical meditation is not the same as meditation in eastern religions. Eastern meditation is not biblical meditation. It can be dangerous and can open up someone's mind for Satan to creep in and attack. I only want to deal with the meaning and blessing of biblical meditation.

Meditation means "the act of focusing one's thoughts: to ponder, think on, muse." It is the act of reflective thinking and contemplation. If meditate or marinate stills seems confusing, think about it this way; as contemplation or reflection.

You read in chapter one how I read 2 Corinthians 12:9 and for months I kept going back to the verse and pondering on it. I kept re-reading it and thinking about it. I was meditating on this verse. Really trying to mine all the truth I could out of it. And through that, the Lord spoke to me.

Biblical meditation should be part of everyone's bible study. It is reading Scripture and focusing on it to find both its meaning and application. We need to reflect on the Word truly give into the Bible study. To meditate on the word effectively you need to incorporate the 3 R's.

READING
REFLECTING
RESPONDING.

When you read a section of the bible you don't need to just jump in anywhere pick out one verse and say this is the answer. You need to read the verses around it or even the entire chapter or book. I have seen this lately quite a bit. People chose a verse that sounds pretty but takes it out of context.

Here are a few examples:

Philippians 4:13 — "I can do all things through Him who gives me strength."

Philippians 4:12 -13– "12 I know what it is to be in need, and I know what it is to have plenty. I have learned the secret of being content in any and every situation, whether well-fed or hungry, whether living in plenty or in want. 13 I can do all things through Him who gives me strength."

It takes on a different meaning now, doesn't it? "I can do all things", is referring to Paul enduring bad times because He is living out his faith no matter what.

> Jeremiah 29:11 — "For I know the plans have for you," declares the Lord, "plans to prosper you and not to harm you, plans to give you hope and a future."

> Jeremiah 29:11-13 — "For I know the plans have for you," declares the Lord, "plans to prosper you and not to harm you, plans to give you hope and a future. Then you will call on me and come and pray to me, and I will listen to you. You will seek me and find me when you seek me with all your heart."

The book of Jeremiah leading up to this point is about Israel's disobedience and God's punishment of them. Chapter 29 is written to the Israelite exiles in Babylon, who were there because of disobedience. These promises are for restoration after judgment with the understanding that discipline will bring the Israelite people to obedience (vs. 12-13). I do not want to rain that kind of fire on myself.

> Galatians 5: 22 – 23- "But the fruit of the Spirit is love, joy, peace, forbearance, kindness, goodness, faithfulness, gentleness, and self-control, Against such things there is no law."

> Galatians 5: 22 – 24– "But the fruit of the Spirit is love, joy, peace, forbearance, kindness, goodness, faithfulness, gentleness, and self-control, Against such things there is no law. Those who belong to Christ Jesus have crucified the flesh with its passions and desires."

I love the fruits of the spirit; however, we have to remember that without the transformation in Christ's image that accompanies being "crucified" such that "I no longer live, yet not I but Christ lives in me." We don't get the fruits without salvation. Christians sure don't want to read the grocery list of sins and bad situations outlined just above these verses, in verses 19-21.

> Matthew 6:33 — "But seek first his kingdom and his righteousness, and all these things will be given to you as well."

> Matthew 5 and 6 — People tend to forget that this verse comes near the end of the Sermon on the Mount. This gives us the beatitudes and detailed information on how Christians should act.

> Ephesians 2:8 – 9 — "For it is by grace you have been saved, through faith—and this is not from yourselves, it is the gift of God— not by works, so that no one can boast."

> Ephesians 2:8 – 10 — "For it is by grace you have been saved, through faith—and this is not from yourselves, it is the gift of God— not

by works, so that no one can boast. For we are God's handiwork, created in Christ Jesus to do good works, which God prepared in advance for us to do."

Absolutely we are saved by grace and it is a gift from God. We tend to want to stop there. If we keep reading, we see that we are saved to serve not saved to sit.

When we reflect on things we look back at them for a deeper meaning. It is important as we reflect on God's Word. We do it with the purpose of learning and growing. As you reflect ensure that you always do it with prayer and humility. Don't ever except God to open up the knowledge storehouses and drop them on you, if you are not spiritually prepared. As you meditate and you read a passage of scripture take time to revisit it. Reread it over and over. Sometimes I will read it out loud or have someone read it to me. Study the scripture. Think about who wrote the book, who was the book for and the time they wrote it. There are many passages in the Bible about sheep and farming. I didn't know anything about that. So I would read a little on the nature of sheep or what it took to sew seeds.

Malachi 3:3 says, "He will sit as a refiner and purifier of silver; he will purify the Levites and refine them like gold and silver. Then the LORD will have men who will bring offerings in righteousness." I knew this verse and one day we were watching PBS it was a show on refining silver. I started to watch how it was done. And that verse took on a whole new meaning for me. To refine and purify silver it must be melted in a boiling furnace. It is removed and the refiner scoops of the impurities that have come to the top. This process of putting the silver in the heat till the impurities come to the top and are scrapped off continues over and over again. As long as it takes, until the silver is pure. I was like, wow! Learning about the traditions and customs during Bible times will allow you to see the Bible through different eyes.

The third R is the response. This is where you examine what you learned and you apply it to your life and situations. You need to ask these questions. How does the word apply to my life: in me personally, in my family, at my workplace, in my church, and in my town? What changes should I make? Or what does this say to me? How can I change to be more of what God wants? Much like the questions for Bible study, these questions will help you to see exactly what God's word is saying.

Probably 80 to 90 percent of the times when God really speaks to me, I have been meditating on something. Normally I am sitting around thinking about a set of scripture, talking about it with family or really studying it. I'll be looking up the original language used or looking at the time and place it was written and then out of left field here comes God's voice. My husband and I were discussing this chapter, and he said, "Yeah, that's when God teaches me the most or shows me something new." To understand how to move forward and allow God to work through you fully and turn battle scars into beauty marks you need to meditate on the word of God. Don't meditate on this book. Go to the Bible and dive in.

Dig Deeper

Take 10 minutes right now meditate on 2 Corinthians 12:9
But he said to me, "My grace is sufficient for you, for my power is made perfect in weakness." Therefore, I will boast all the more gladly about my weaknesses, so that Christ's power may rest on me.
Here is a little background to think on.
Author: Paul
Time: Around 55 to 60 AD. 2 Corinthians may have been written from Macedonia from information in 2 Corinthians 2:13 and 7:5.
Who it is written to: The church at Corinth.

Read 2 Corinthians 12: 1 – 10

I must go on boasting. Although there is nothing to be gained, I will go on to visions and revelations from the Lord. ² I know a man in Christ who fourteen years ago was caught up to the third heaven. Whether it was in the body or out of the body I do not know—God knows. ³ And I know that this man—whether in the body or apart from the body I do not know, but God knows— ⁴ was caught up to paradise and heard inexpressible things, things that no one is permitted to tell. ⁵ I will boast about a man like that, but I will not boast about myself, except about my weaknesses. ⁶ Even if I should choose to boast, I would not be a fool, because I would be speaking the truth. But I refrain, so no one will think more of me than is warranted by what I do or say, ⁷ or because of these surpassingly great revelations. Therefore, in order to keep me from becoming conceited, I was given a thorn in my flesh, a messenger of Satan, to torment me. [8] Three times I pleaded with the Lord to take it away from me. [9] But he said to me, "My grace is sufficient for you, for my power is made perfect in weakness." Therefore I will boast all the more gladly about my weaknesses, so that Christ's power may rest on me. [10] That is why, for Christ's sake, I delight in weaknesses, in insults, in hardships, in persecutions, in difficulties. For when I am weak, then I am strong.

Has God put a verse or passage on your heart that you just keep thinking about?

What is it?

_____

_____

_____

_____

This week, take time in your quiet time and examine this verse meditate on it.

Think about this verse or verses and delve into its meaning.

Read the verse and pray about it at least twice a day.

Record everything you learned and what God is telling you.

Pray that God will give you insight and knowledge about how these verses affect you.

Chapter 6 - Follow God's Prescription

So far, I hope that you have identified some of your battle scars, prayed for healing and help, studied the Bible for direction and meditated on the word for understanding. You may be thinking I still hurt, I still feel weak, or I still don't feel like God has given me answers. It's okay. At the beginning of this Bible study I told you, God took me on a journey. The thing about journeys is that they take time. It took me months almost a year before I really felt like boasting in my weaknesses. And still, after a year or to some things are still hard to tell people about.

I suffer from horrible self-esteem. It started as a kid who was weird and didn't see the world the way everyone else did. It didn't help that I have chronic bad hair and believed I was not good at anything. I had to study so hard to get C's and people around me got A's and never opened a book. I was talked about and bullied all the way through school and it didn't help that from the 6th grade until I was 21 I had one boyfriend. It lasted for about 2 weeks. I did ask a guy to my senior prom he told me no. The terrible thing was he was one of my best friends. All of these things and much more made me believe that I was not worth anything. It is this wound that Satan plays on more than anything else. I have made many bad decisions in my life and Satan will try to get in my head and make me second guess everything I do. He will tell me things like; you are not good enough and everyone will laugh at you. I battle this every day. And I have to throw the Bible at Satan.

Genesis 1:27

> So God created mankind in his own image, in the image of God he created them; male and female he created them.

Psalm 139:13-18

> For you created my inmost being; you knit me together in my mother's womb. [14] I praise you because I am fearfully and wonderfully made;your works are wonderful, I know that full well. [15] My frame was not hidden from you when I was made in the secret place, when I was woven together in the depths of the earth. [16] Your eyes saw my unformed body; all the days ordained for me were written in your book before one of them came to be. [17] How precious to me are your thoughts, God How vast is the sum of them! [18] Were I to count them, they would outnumber the grains of sand—when I awake, I am still with you.

Using scripture to battle Satan in a powerful thing. Jesus used scripture to battle Satan when He was tempted in the wilderness. We should use it as well. Jesus is always the perfect example to follow. When we use the scripture as Jesus did; Satan has no way to fight back.

So as your studying and strengthening yourself for God's work, write down and memorize verses that help you fight

Satan's arrows. My husband used to be shy and was scared to death to be in front of people. We used to laugh and say, "If I had a superpower I would be the human shield." He would frequently use me as a shield if we had to be in front of people or if there was a ceremony or public speaking, I would do the speaking while he handed out things or ran the sound or projection. He was even terrified to pray in church. I would frequently quote 2 Timothy 1:7 "For God has not given us a spirit of fear and timidity, but of power, love, and self-discipline." Over time, he did change. He starred in many plays and has prayed in church. He still works on power and fear. I quoted this so much to he that it started being ingrained in my son and he started coming out of his shell. In fact, we are just about to perform a passion play in which we all have parts.

To follow God's prescription, you need to be ready to use prayer, bible study and everything that God gives you to fight Satan. There is a reason the Bible says, "Put on the whole armor of God." You need to use it all. How good would a soldier be if he had no armor or shield and was only equipped with one dagger? Let's face it the reasons for most of our battle scars is because we were not suited up in the armor of God when we went out.

On this journey from battle scars to beauty marks, you need to suit up every day. The road is long and the more you heal, the more Satan is going to try to wound you more. One of my favorite songs to listen to before my quiet time is Casting Crowns, " Until the Whole World Hears." because it says, "Let us shine the light of Jesus in the darkest night Ready yourselves, ready yourselves May the powers of darkness tremble as our praises rise." To get ready to follow Jesus, let armor up and prepare for the battle ahead.

45

Ephesians 6:10-18

> Finally, be strong in the Lord and in his mighty power. [11] Put on the full armor of God, so that you can take your stand against the devil's schemes. [12] For our struggle is not against flesh and blood, but against the rulers, against the authorities, against the powers of this dark world and against the spiritual forces of evil in the heavenly realms. [13] Therefore put on the full armor of God, so that when the day of evil comes, you may be able to stand your ground, and after you have done everything, to stand. [14] Stand firm then, with the belt of truth buckled around your waist, with the breastplate of righteousness in place, [15] and with your feet fitted with the readiness that comes from the gospel of peace. [16] In addition to all this, take up the shield of faith, with which you can extinguish all the flaming arrows of the evil one. [17] Take the helmet of salvation and the sword of the Spirit, which is the word of God.
>
> [18] And pray in the Spirit on all occasions with all kinds of prayers and requests. With this in mind, be alert and always keep on praying for all the Lord's people.

To get ready to follow Jesus you must get dressed. Let's take a moment and look at how to do that. The first thing is what to wear. These verses lay out exactly what to wear.

» The Belt of Truth
» The Breastplate of Righteousness

- » The Gospel Shoes of Peace
- » The Shield of Faith
- » The Helmet of Salvation
- » And the Sword of the Spirit

God gives us these weapons and armor to keep us safe and help us to endure the battle (remember life is a battle). What are these weapons and armor and how do we use them?

Put on the Belt of Truth!

This belt is not that rhinestone number you have in the top of your closet. A soldier's belt in Bible times was a girdle and coverage to protect the soldiers' lower abdominal organs and business or private parts. This belt also holds the tunic down and to holster weapons for easy access. Our spiritual belt is in our truth or integrity and holds our faith in and keeps weapons ready. Without the belt of truth every day, you will lose your battle against evil.

I can go to church every time the door opens and serve God at every opportunity, but don't love and treat others with respect; I am not living with integrity? If you give to the poor but lie constantly, are you living with integrity? Put on the belt of truth.

Put on the Breastplate of Righteousness!

A breastplate covers the soldiers' lungs, heart, and vital organs. For a Christian, this is made of righteousness or purity. Satan wants to defile you and make you corrupt. It makes him happy when he tempts you with the immorality that exists in the world today. Movies, TV, the internet, advertisements, and songs with filthy situations that are designed to tempt you.

Keep yourself safe with purity and righteousness. Wearing the breastplate of righteousness will guard your heart against sin.

Put on the Shoes of the Gospel of Peace!

The soldiers during Paul's time wore shoes with tacks on the bottom, like cleats. These keep them steady and keep them from slipping. The Gospel of peace is the Gospel of Jesus Christ. When we steady ourselves on the Gospel it is like sticking those spikes in the ground, and we are immovable. Philippians 4: 7 says "And the peace of God, which transcends all understanding, will guard your hearts and your minds in Christ Jesus."

When Satan tries to knock us down, we need to rely on the Gospel of peace.

Pick up the Shield of Faith!

Shields are used to stop attacks and push back on the enemy. One of the many jobs for shields during this time was to protect from arrows. You can guarantee that Satan is going to fire arrows at you. Some arrows include; temptation, sickness, feelings of doubt, discouragement, hurt, etc. Using your shield of faith makes you ready for what he throws at you and will protect you from flaming arrows.

> Ephesians 6:16 says, "in addition to all this, take up the shield of faith, with which you can extinguish all the flaming arrows of the evil one."

Put on the Helmet of Salvation!

The helmet of salvation is to guard your mind. If your head becomes wounded, you may not be able to think or strategize. Wounds to the head can also be fatal. Satan is going to try to put thoughts in our mind. Hold fast to your salvation and fill your mind with scriptures, worship music, Christian friends and your Bible.

Pull Out the Sword of the Spirit

The Sword of the Spirit is the Word of God. As I said before the Bible is the word of God and it is good for many applications. This is why it is the weapon. It can help you be a better Christian, fight of Satan and witness to an unbeliever at the same time. The Bible is the Christians Swiss army knife. It can feed you and fight for you. It is the strongest weapon God gave us.

Hebrews 4:12

> "For the word of God is alive and active. Sharper than any double-edged sword, it penetrates even to dividing soul and spirit, joints and marrow; it judges the thoughts and attitudes of the heart."

Now none of us can stand in our closet saying, "I have nothing to wear." God has given us a full set of armor.

Dig Deeper

Step back and take a moment and reread Ephesians 6:10-18

Are there any pieces of your armor that are weathered or torn?

_____

_____

_____

_____

Could your weapon be stronger or sharper?

_____

_____

_____

What are some things you can do or change that will make your armor of God stronger?

_____

_____

_____

_____

This week, try to make those changes in your life.

When you get up every morning read Ephesians 6:10-18 and say a little prayer. Then turn back here and write down all the things that changed or what was different.

Pray that God would strengthen your armor to ready yourselves to follow him.

Chapter 7 - What do I do?

I often hear "I don't know God's will for my life." In fact, I have said that very statements a few times. We frequently get so bogged down with trying to figure out God's will or plan for us that we overlook the obvious. It's like the old saying, "You can't see the forest for the trees." Figuring out what God wants you to do and that the first step is can be daunting. We don't want to move before God is ready, but we also don't want to miss an opportunity either. Left to my own devices, I make many wrong decisions and stumble off down wrong paths. So deciding what to do to follow God's will was a terrifying thought for me. I made a string of notoriously wrong decisions in my twenties, mostly because Missy lived for that wretched fleshy part, not for God. And there were a few years there that I would say yes to just about anything for fear of hurting someone's feelings or because I was afraid they would not love me. What I learned from that time in my life is that I should not be left to my own devices.

The great thing is that God never abandoned me to fend for myself. I did that all on my own. The entire time I was out there making bad choices God had told me everything I needed to know in the Bible I was just too stubborn to read it. You see, God has a plan for all of us, that is part of God's will. But there is another part of God's will in that He wants us to be the best and most productive Christians we can. This part of God's will, He has lined out for us in the Bible. So what do I do? Do what you know is right. Do what the Bible tells you to do. Start to make a genuine effort to put into practice what the Bible says. This helps you become lined up with God's will. For me, this required a complete clean out of my old life. I had to refocus my life around God.

To start this look at what Jesus told us to do. If you want to get yourself in line with God's will, start with the basics. Start living how God intends for us to live. Jesus tells us this in Matthew.

Matthew 22:36-40

> "Teacher, which is the greatest commandment in the Law?"
>
> [37] Jesus replied: "'Love the Lord your God with all your heart and with all your soul and with all your mind.' [38] This is the first and greatest commandment. [39] And the second is like it: 'Love your neighbor as yourself.' [40] All the Law and the Prophets hang on these two commandments."

To really get down to the nitty-gritty in these verses, we need to meditate on them and mine all the info we can out of them. The first thing Jesus says is 'Love the Lord your God.' Love is interesting because the Greeks have six different words for love while we just have the one. And frankly, it is thrown around so often that it has lost its meaning. We say things like: I love that shirt or I love DR Pepper or I love my family or I love God. Do you really love DR. Pepper as much as God or your family? I hope not. The Greek terms for love denote different types of love. The six Greek words for love are Agape, Eros, Philia, Storge, Pragma, and Xenia. Each is distinctive from the other. Here Jesus uses agape. Agape is defined as God's love for man and man's love for God. This is a sacrificial love that expects nothing in return. It is the love God shows us. The love that sent Jesus to die for sins. It is a love that does not require or expect anything in return. Start to love the Lord your God with a love that is sacrificial and expects nothing in return. This means we willingly and cheerfully sacrifice time, money, talents and anything else for God. That is hard enough with our wretched fleshy self peeking its head up. But it does not stop there.

The next bit is even more "with all your heart." I was thinking, "Oh, I got this." you may be thinking that as well. I love God with all my heart. Let's take a minute and look at the heart. The Greek word is Kardia, which is where we get cardiac. This is defined as the organ in the body, but also, the center of one's physical and spiritual life. The center of our lives. When we think about our spiritual lives the heart is where we keep our loves, our desires, our hopes, our dreams, and our passions. We are called by Jesus to love God with all our hearts with a sacrificial type of love. So we are to turn over our loves, our desires, our hopes, our dreams and our passions to God. Whoa! That is the whole shebang. Yes, it is. When we start to do this our will takes a turn and God's will becomes our will. We began to treasure things we never did before and things that seemed so vital are minimal.

As we continue, we need to love God "with all your soul." Soul in Greek is Psuche. It means the breath of life or the vital force that animates our bodies. Your soul is the part of you that will live forever. FOREVER! Everyone's soul lives forever the saved will live with God and Jesus and the unbelievers will live forever in hell with Satan and his minions. Your soul is the most important part of your body. This earthly body will fade away, but the soul endures forever. This means that you love God with that piece if you that Jesus saved and will live forever. Loving God with all your soul requires you feed your soul regularly and think of the eternal benefits before the physical.

"With all your mind." This is the last way that Jesus says to love God. Mind is Greek is Dianoia. This is the faculty of understanding, feeling and thinking. So why do we need to love God with all our mind? Satan attacks our minds more than any other parts of our body. He makes us question things or shoots some evil thoughts in there. Not to mention the doubts and lustful thoughts. When we love God with all our minds, we use His word for understanding and rely on Him to help with our feelings, and we think on good and holy things instead of the wretched things of the flesh. So read this way we need to start Loving God with a sacrificial love in every aspect of our life. We need to love him everywhere at all times with everything inside of us no matter what our situation is.

We are not done yet Jesus is still talking. 'Love your neighbor as yourself.' This one is pretty easy to understand, but hard to do. Love here is agape just as before sacrificial love. So we are to sacrificially love everyone as you love yourself. I was asked last Sunday how do you love someone you can't stand. This is the beauty of agape. Agape love is not linked to any emotions. It is linked to actions. You can show someone agape and not be particularly fond of them or their actions. However one of the best ways I have learned to love people, who are hard to love, is to remember they are a soul with a body. Look at their soul. Find the things in them that God put there. Find their gifts and talents. And always pray for that person. When you can do that you find it easier to love them because you're seeing what God sees. The beauty God put there.

This is the kicking off point it is not all you should do, but it is where to start. Once you are working hard on these and doing your quiet time you may feel led to do something else. Just remember if God tells you to do it in the Bible such as feed to hungry or care for the orphans, you don't need to question it if it is right to do it.

Remember James 4:17 "**If anyone, then, knows the good they ought to do and doesn't do it, it is sin for them.**" So if you know it is right, do it. No one ever changed the world or did anything of value waiting. One of my favorite songs to get me going and jazzed about the day is Matthew West's Do Something. The lyrics say, "I woke up this morning, saw a world full of trouble now, I thought, how'd we ever get so far down, and how's it ever going to turn around. So I turned my eyes to Heaven. I thought, "God, why don't you do something?" Well, I just couldn't bear the thought of people living in poverty, children sold into slavery. The thought disgusted me. So, I shook my fist at Heaven said, "God, why don't you do something?" He said, "I did, yeah, I created you" If not us, then who. If not me and you right now, it's time for us to do something, if not now, then when will we see an end to all this pain it's not enough to do nothing. It's time for us to do something." We know what to do stop waiting on a burning bush or God to smack you across the head with a crow ball. Just do what you know is right.

Dig Deeper

Take a minute and think about your loves, desires, hopes, dreams, and passions. Do you have some you need to turn to God?

List them here.

_____

_____

_____

_____

Is there something God has put on your heart and you know it is good but you have not done it? If so, what is it?

_____

_____

_____

_____

Do you have areas of your life where you are still trying to keep control of? If so, ask God to help you let go of them.

_____

_____

_____

_____

Every day this next week do something you know is right but you haven't done. (EX. Take cookies to a neighbor, visit a widow or the nursing home, call a friend you know is hurting and pray with them.)

List ideas here.

1. _____
2. _____
3. _____
4. _____
5. _____
6. _____
7. _____

Continue your quiet time and add those people you are going to reach out to your prayer list.

Pray and ask God to lead you to Bible passages that will help you do what God wants you to do.

Chapter 8 - Stop Doing What You are not Supposed to do. (Stop Being Nasty)

A couple of years ago my husband were teaching a group of teenage boys. Twice a month they would stay after church on Sunday, I would cook lunch, we would do a Bible study and my husband would teach them handyman skills they used to do service for the church. Like most teenagers, they had good intentions but would make bad choices sometimes. When they would say something or do something inappropriate, I just started saying, "Stop being nasty." It was their cue that what they were doing was wrong. After a while, every time I said it everyone in the room stopped doing what they were doing and thought, "Is she talking to me?" Then I was asked to teach a True Love Waits program at our church, our boys attended, and when I would talk about what we shouldn't do they would yell "Stop being nasty." It became such a thing that the password for our Wi-Fi for a while was "stopbeingnasty316." it has been changed since so don't try. I have even caught my son telling people to stop being nasty. This little saying has become a trigger in all our lives now. It seems quite funny but it helped us to say, "Hey you are sinning stop that" in a way that gets someone's attention without hurting their feelings. As Christians, we sometimes forget that we not only need to do good. We also need to stop sinning. Romans 3:23 is a constant

reminder " for all have sinned and fall short of the glory of God."
We are all going to sin because no one is perfect except Jesus
Christ. However, we can strive to live as sinless as possible.

It is so easy for us to say, "I don't feel God's Presence," or
"God doesn't talk to me." More times than not we have such
sin in our lives that we have built a wall between ourselves and
God. During the dark years when I was running from God, I
had un-confessed sin and sins that I just keep doing over and
over. These sins created a wall between me and God. I was
comfortable in my sin and that was dangerous. I had stopped
listening to the Holy Spirits convictions. My life was going
to be my way, I would do what I wanted to do and I didn't
care. This did not turn out well for me. The entire time I was
angry, frustrated and would fight anyone at any time. Why? I
missed my relationship with God. Nevertheless, my fleshy self
was winning. The reason I didn't hear God's voice or feel his
presence was my sin. I had to come back and ask for forgiveness
and repent. When I did that, God's love melted that wall. Sin
in your life will make you feel isolated and unloved. God will
never leave you and he always loves you. It is you that has to ask
forgiveness and take the step to tear down the wall.

When I have to deal with sin in my own life, I often think
of Gideon. Yes. That Gideon. His story is in Judges 6-8. We are
only going to look at a part at the beginning of the story. God
used Gideon to help free the Israelites from the Midianites. God
chose him for a mighty deed. He was called to save an entire
nation. But before God could make Gideon a mighty warrior,
he had to get right.

Judges 6: 25-27

> That same night the Lord said to him, "Take
> the second bull from your father's herd, the one

seven years old. Tear down your father's altar to Baal and cut down the Asherah pole beside it. [26] Then build a proper kind of altar to the LORD your God on the top of this height. Using the wood of the Asherah pole that you cut down, offer the second bull as a burnt offering."

[27] So Gideon took ten of his servants and did as the LORD told him. But because he was afraid of his family and the townspeople, he did it at night rather than in the daytime.

Before Gideon could do the amazing things God had planned for him. He had to get his house in order literally. He had to tear down his idols and make a sacrifice to God. We don't have to offer burnt sacrifices anymore because of Jesus' sacrifice for us, but we do need to confess and repent. There are times in all of our lives that we have to take out the trash. If I am honest, I am trying to clean up and take out the trash on a daily basis. I don't believe my spiritual house will ever be spotless, because I am not perfect, but I steadily try to work on it. Proverbs 28:13 says, "Whoever conceals their sins does not prosper, but the one who confesses and renounces them finds mercy" Mercy is not getting a punishment you deserve. God gives us mercy when we confess and turn away from our sin. But those people that hide their sin and never confess it, they will not prosper.

Sometimes I think of our lives like a house. Before we are Christians, Jesus stands outside waiting to come in. Patiently waiting on us to be ready. When we get saved we open the door and let Jesus in. So many times, we stick Jesus in one room of our house. Usually the one with the big window facing the street. You know the one room that is always cleaned for visitors. It might even have the covers over the furniture. To the world, we are showing off our Jesus. He smiles and waves at the passersby. However, we refuse to let him see the rest of the house. The parts of the house we haven't managed to clean up yet. Jesus wants to roam the house freely and doesn't just want to be visited on Sunday and Wednesday. So we need to open the doors and let Jesus come in and help us to clean out the house. Yes! Even that closet or spare bedroom that seems to collect all the junk we don't want anyone to see. Let Jesus help you clean your spiritual house.

> James4:7-10 says, "Submit yourselves, then, to God. Resist the devil, and he will flee from you. [8] Come near to God and he will come near to you. Wash your hands, you sinners, and purify your hearts, you double-minded. [9] Grieve, mourn and wail. Change your laughter to mourning and your joy to gloom. [10] Humble yourselves before the Lord, and he will lift you up." Cleaning up your house will probably be more painful than anticipated. We are supposed to feel sorrow for the sin we committed. It is all right to sit down and cry from time to time. We caused pain to god with our sin. There is no reason that we should not have feelings of sadness and shame from that. This spiritual clean up will be painful. We start by trying to identify our sins and work to fight temptation. You are probably going to feel regret, shame and even sorrow for the sins you've committed. You are not alone. Everyone has sin and everyone need God to hold on to when they are working to get that sin out.

You may stop doing a sin, but Satan is still going to tempt you and you need God to fight those temptations.

In 2 Corinthians 7:9-10, Paul says, "yet now I am happy, not because you were made sorry, but because your sorrow led you to repentance. For you became sorrowful as God intended and so were not harmed in any way by us. [10] Godly sorrow brings repentance that leads to salvation and leaves no regret, but worldly sorrow brings death."

Everyone sins. We know that we have all sinned and fallen short of the Glory of God. So while you are preparing yourself for the transformation that God has for you from battles scars to beauty marks, stop being nasty! Stop doing what you know as sin. You may know not to lie, cheat, steal, commit adultery or murder. They are many sins listed in the Bible. Below is a list of just a few.

Galatians 5:19-21

"The acts of the flesh are obvious: sexual immorality, impurity and debauchery; [20] idolatry and witchcraft; hatred, discord, jealousy, fits of rage, selfish ambition, dissensions, factions [21] and envy; drunkenness, orgies, and the like. I warn you, as I did before, that those who live like this will not inherit the kingdom of God."

To completely live for God, you can't live comfortably in your sin. You need to be striving to live better every day. God sees your deeds, and He sees you working on that sin. If you ask for His help, He will help you to fight temptations and cleanse you. If you ask God to convict you of your sin you are living comfortably with, He will. But for all this to help you start healing, you must be willing to change. You have to decide you are ready to change. No one can decide to change you, but you.

Dig Deeper

This is a painful part of the process, but think about your life and list any un-confessed or unrepentant sins here. If you are embarrassed or ashamed, think about them.

_____

_____

_____

_____

Stop right now while they are on your mind and pray to confess them and ask the Lord for help.

Make a conscious effort in the next week to work on these sins. When temptation strikes or you feel this sin boiling up find a distraction or pray for help at that moment.

> Every day this week read James4:7-10 says, "Submit yourselves, then, to God. Resist the devil, and he will flee from you. [8] Come near to God and he will come near to you. Wash your hands, you sinners, and purify your hearts, you double-minded. [9] Grieve, mourn and wail. Change your laughter to mourning and your joy to gloom. [10] Humble yourselves before the Lord, and he will lift you up."

Pray again and ask God to guard your heart against temptation or to convict you of the sin you already have in there.

Chapter 9 - Lift Others Up Instead of Tearing Them Down

You might think didn't we already talked about what to do and not to do. Yes, we did. However, in the world, today adoration or lifting someone up is being seen less and less. With social media the way it is. Someone will get slightly upset at someone, go online, and tear up another's reputation without a thought. I have seen it more and more. Behind a computer screen, people can be ruthless. This is nothing new. People have been negative and attacking others for centuries. This is why lifting up others gets its own chapter. Lifting people up is what we are supposed to do. However, sometimes we struggle with this act. Even though it is a critical part of loving your neighbor as yourself.

Sister Night is a ministry my church does once a year. It is a free night for women to come to eat a free meal, hear a bible study, listen and worship with amazing singers and hear the word of God. I have been blessed to deliver the Bible study for the last two years and one of the singer/ speakers is a wonderful Christian lady I have been blessed to have known since 1st grade, Patricia Wright. Tricia was speaking to the ladies about Matthew 5:13-16.

> "You are the salt of the earth. But if the salt loses its saltiness, how can it be made salty again?

It is no longer good for anything, except to be thrown out and trampled underfoot.

[14] "You are the light of the world. A town built on a hill cannot be hidden. [15] Neither do people light a lamp and put it under a bowl. Instead they put it on its stand, and it gives light to everyone in the house. [16] In the same way, let your light shine before others, that they may see your good deeds and glorify your Father in heaven."

She was telling the ladies that we as Christians are the salt of the earth. But at times we don't act like it towards other people. We talk negatively, gossip or completely break someone's spirit because of selfish desires. So when you start to feel this way or when another woman begins to be negative just say, "Pass the Salt." In our family or our church family, we hear it quite often. Someone will yell across the fellowship hall or even in Wal-Mart "Pass The Salt." My sister and I joke about it getting so bad sometimes we have to pass the pepper as or that we need to hit each other in the head with the shaker. To be honest, it is not that bad, but we do rib each other quite a bit. Pass the Salt has become like stop being nasty. A nice way of saying, take a minute and think before you speak.

We are living in a narcissistic, selfie driven society; where sarcasm and building yourself up at someone else's expense has become a way of life. Everything about that is wrong. Love your neighbor. Love as defined in 1 Corinthians 13 and most of the words to define love are about you caring for others. For example, love is kind. The very definition of kind is to put another's well-being before yours. How many times in the last month have you done this? Not for your family or spouse but for others.

Being bold enough to speak up and stop the verbal destruction of someone's character is hard. As a Christian, it is often the right thing to do. But it should always be done in love and with scripture. At a ladies group I went to, every week we would come together, and before long someone was asking if we had seen this Facebook post or did we hear about so-and-so. As we are community driven people, we would get sucked in and it would snowball and before long the mob mentality was sitting in, and we would be all upset over something that may or may not have happened. The Holy Spirit started convicting me about this and it came to me to avoid this talk all together. I started just saying, "That's none of my business" or "not my circus, not my monkeys." The ladies started not telling me these things. This was a battle God and I won because I came to him and asked for help.

Working in various church kitchens, I would hear snide remarks about people getting in the front of the line or how much food they ate. At one point in my life, I could not get 1 John 4: 7-8 out of my head. In the verses John says, "Dear friends, let us love one another, for love comes from God. Everyone who loves has been born of God and knows God. [8] Whoever does not love does not know God, because God is love." God was really working on me to love. Over and over again, daily, I would hear love. After a while, hearing these comments from Christian ladies and gentlemen would just hurt me. When finally God would not let me stand there anymore. I smiled and said, "If they are hungry feed them if they are naked clothe them." The looks that were given to me were probably in my top ten list of stink eyes. But again they would stop.

This happens everywhere. Working with the youth we

would have kids that would come for a while mess up and go to Juvenal hall or fall out of the church and come back. Over and over again with the same things. I was listening to some adults complaining about having this kid back at church after he cursed, was violent, and acted stupidly the last time he was there. I said, "God forgave me. How can I not forgive him." and "I would say things like, God has given me four or five chances. So I should give chances to others." God helped me to say these things in love I tried never to say these things sarcastically; always with love in a quiet voice. My goal was to lovingly direct them back to the Bible. If you speak God's truth, no one can stand against you. They may have talked about me when I walked off. I honestly don't mind. God gave me the strength to stand up for those people to my friends. God can for you too, if you come at it with a heart of love for the lost and broken of the world.

When a mother walks into church with a bunch of screaming kids and her hair's all a mess, there is a spit up stain on her shirt, and she looks like she has slept in a week, don't run up to her and direct her to the nursery right away or switch pews because kids annoy you. Go up to her hug her neck and tell her how much you appreciate her for bringing those kids to church to learn of God's love ask her if she needs help and play with the kids. If a drunk that smells of alcohol walks in don't shun him or scoot away from him, hug him, shake his hand, and offer to sit next to him. The church is a hospital for the sinners not a waiting room for the self-righteous.

Now that you stopped tearing down and you are passing the salt, you need to lift others up. And don't just mean in prayer. Lifting people up in prayer is important. But encouraging and edifying a person is an entirely different bag of worms. Being around encouraging people can make the bitterest people peep up. I have seen people on the edge of being burnt out rekindle their flame by one or two people saying, "Thank you." We don't serve God for thanks on earth, but we are called to encourage others. I have personally seen people with magnificent talents and gifts get their spirits crushed by negative criticism. People that could sing, but refused to, because someone remarked about them being off-key, or they didn't like the song. Are we serious? What about Hebrews 3:13 "But encourage one another daily, as long as it is called "Today," so that none of you may be hardened by sin's deceitfulness." Or Ephesians 4:11-16

> "So Christ himself gave the apostles, the prophets, the evangelists, the pastors and teachers, [12] to equip his people for works of service, so that the body of Christ may be built up [13] until we all reach unity in the faith and in the knowledge of the Son of God and become mature, attaining to the whole measure of the fullness of Christ.

> [14] Then we will no longer be infants, tossed back and forth by the waves, and blown here and there by every wind of teaching and by the cunning and craftiness of people in their deceitful scheming. [15] Instead, speaking the truth in love, we will grow to become in every respect the mature body of him who is the head, that is, Christ. [16] From him the whole body, joined and held together by every supporting ligament, grows and builds itself up in love, as each part does its work."

An encouraging word can fuel a person's gift and talent and it can bloom into a wonderful service of God. Learning to lift others up and to support people in their ministry strengthens the entire body of Christ. The thought of crushing someone's spirit or causing someone not to serve God scares me. I don't wanna stand in front of God and answer for that. You know the saying one butterfly flapping its wings across the globe can start a hurricane. In the same way, one person in line with God following God's command can start a revival. I don't want to be the person that stops the revival because of my critical words.

There are a few things you can do push yourself to be an encourager. Think of others higher or better than yourself. People in leadership positions that build up the people on their team and put them first build a team with high regards for one other and the leader. Be humble in all you do. Think before you speak. Always think about how you build someone up and try to make sure there are no underhanded remarks or sarcasm. Praise people whether you think they deserve it or not. If they are serving God or praising God, feed that desire to serve. Be quick to forgive and remember that you need forgiveness at times too. Keep others secrets, don't lie and never gossip. Not only is it the right thing to do it also builds your integrity so people believe you when you admonish them. Share information, scripture or books that could build up or expand the gifts or talents a person has. Be positive. Positivity breeds positivity and vice versa. Love always. 1 Corinthians 13: 4-8 &13 says, "Love is patient, love is kind. It does not envy, it does not boast, it is not proud. It is not rude, it is not self-seeking, it is not easily angered, and it keeps no record of wrongs. Love does not delight in evil but rejoices with the truth. It always protects, always trusts, always hopes, and always perseveres. Love never fails ... And now these three remain faith, hope, and love. But the greatest of these is love." Love people for the eternal soul that they have not the fleshy body that is a temporary host for the soul.

Dig Deeper

Think of how many times in the last month you should have "Passed the Salt."

Are there similarities in these times? Did they happen with the same people? Did they happen in the same places?

_____

_____

_____

_____

Make a conscious effort this week to pray a simple prayer when you are in those situations again. Ask God to edit your tongue and show love.

Think of seven people you know that needs encouragement. It could be in their job, their service to God, their talents, family life or their calling.

1. _____
2. _____
3. _____
4. _____
5. _____
6. _____
7. _____

Remember Hebrews 3:13 "But encourage one another day after day, as long as it is still called "Today," so that none of you will be hardened by the deceitfulness of sin."

Pray for these people each day and ask for God to give you the words for them.

Choose one person a day and encourage them. Go by and see them. Give them a call or text. Send them a message on social media or email; send them a card in the mail or etc.

Every day read 1 Corinthians 13 and be reminded of what love is.

Pray for God to use you to encourage others to do good works and build God's kingdom.

Chapter 10 - Stop Picking Your Scabs

I grew up outside a small town in East Texas. We lived in the country. The forest or woods around our house was our playground. There were trees, lakes, clearings and plenty of wildlife. So to say we got bumps and bruises would be an understatement. We frequently got scraps and cuts while we were playing. When we got home mom would tend to our wounds and make us feel better. I was a fidgety child that frequently picked at scabs. If my mom said it once, she said a thousand times, "If you keep picking your scabs, they will never heal!" If you keep picking at scabs, they will leave a scar. As a Christian, we pick our scabs when we don't forgive. When we don't forgive others or can't forgive ourselves.

One thing I noticed during the dark years was my inability to forgive. I was vengeful and angry. I was once told by someone I love that I was and I quote, "The most hateful person I have ever met." that cut deep and I still remember that moment vividly. Forgiving myself was too hard, so why forgive others. When I went back to God, I found it easy to forgive others for what they had done. But I still wrestle with forgiving myself at times. Forgiveness means to start with a clean slate, to pardon, or to cancel a debt. So essentially we are saying I forgive you and I wish no harm or hurt to you and I want only happiness for you. But do you even think that about you? Or are you still picking the scabs?

At times, and by that, I mean most of the time; I am my own worst critic. I beat myself up long after I have been forgiven. And the more I speak openly with people the more I realize that many people suffer the same affliction. Repentance is an important facet of a Christian's life. God's word also tells us we need to learn from our mistakes and move on. The Bible says that God is a forgiving God. He forgives us of our sins and trespasses first. He reminds that learning to forgive includes learning to forgive ourselves.

Matthew 6:14-15

> "For if you forgive other people when they sin against you, your heavenly Father will also forgive you. 15 But if you do not forgive others their sins, your Father will not forgive your sins."

1 John 1:9

> "e confess our sins, he is faithful and just and will forgive us our sins and purify us from all unrighteousness."

Colossians 3:13

> "Bear with each other and forgive one another if any of you has a grievance against someone. Forgive as the Lord forgave you."

Forgiving someone is not something you do for them. Forgiveness is something you need to do for you. I was once speaking to a teenage girl who had been abused by her grandfather and her parents refused to believe her. She said that she didn't know how to forgive them for the pain they had caused. I had to explain that Satan was in this world corrupting people and that unfortunately is something we have to live with. It was not her fault this happened, but she had to get to a place where she didn't wish harm or retribution on her family. She blamed herself for allowing it to go on for years. We talked prayed and read scripture for about 2 hours trying to grasp the concept of forgiveness. These are some verses we read and prayed on.

Ephesians 4:31-32

> "Get rid of all bitterness, rage and anger, brawling and slander, along with every form of malice. [32] Be kind and compassionate to one another, forgiving each other, just as in Christ God forgave you."

Luke 17:3-4

> "If your brother or sister sins against you, rebuke them; and if they repent, forgive them. [4] Even if they sin against you seven times in a day and seven times come back to you saying 'I repent,' you must forgive them.'."

Luke 7:47

> "Therefore, I tell you, her many sins have been forgiven—as her great love has shown. But whoever has been forgiven little loves little."

Mark 11:25

> "²⁵ And when you stand praying, if you hold anything against anyone, forgive them, so that your Father in heaven may forgive you your sins."

We can talk about forgiveness all day, but we can't figure out how to forgive ourselves and others, what good is it. Where do we start? Identify someone you need to forgive or a situation you need to forgive yourself for. I don't think this is hard for all of us, but if you are having trouble ask the following questions.

Does something I did or something someone did to me keep coming up in my mind?

Do I feel anger or bitterness about a situation or someone?

Do I seek retribution or delight when something bad happens to someone?

Do I feel shame and grief over things I have done?

Do I often tell others how someone mistreated me?

Did you answer "yes" to any of the questions? Then there's probably someone that needs to be forgiven. Once the identity of the person or situation is known to you. Are you willing to do the work to forgive them? I didn't ask you if they deserved forgiveness. I asked if you were willing to do it. Make a decision right now, to forgive. Remember Ephesians 4:32, "Be kind and compassionate to one another, forgiving each other, just as in Christ God forgave you."

Forgive yourselves and others as soon as possible. Bitterness and unforgiveness are like an acid that corrodes you from the inside out. It takes hold of you and makes it harder to forgive. If the scar you or someone caused you to have is a deep large scar, you may find it hard to forgive right off the bat. When this happens, it is okay to ask God for assistance. God understands bitterness and anger. He knows your heart and if you are willing to say I need to forgive. He will help you find ways to make it easier.

There are times when you need to go you to a person and tell them you forgive them. Especially if they are having trouble forgiving themselves. But many times forgiveness should be done in private. I have often been hurt by people that I honestly don't believe they meant to hurt me. (At least I hope so.) To bring this up to them might cause them pain and that is not what I want to do. There is no need to make it public every time you forgive someone. My son has autism and is very much a rule follower. He just can't let go when people cheat or break the rules. He wants to shout and bring it back up for days, even months. It was so hard to teach him about forgiveness. Because he was out for vengeance over the smallest infraction. We came up with a few sayings to help him to get to a point where he wanted to forgive. We would say, "It is okay to let people be wrong." or "They have the right to be in the wrong." We need to remember this when we want to run into the church and confront a church lady with, "You did such and such to me, but I forgive you." Just consider if this situation is on their heart enough that knowing they have your forgiveness helps. When considering whether it is right to tell someone you forgive them to consider these verses:

Proverbs 10:12

> Hatred stirs up conflict, but love covers over all wrongs.

Proverbs 12:16

> A fool shows his annoyance at once, but a
> prudent man overlooks an insult.

Proverbs 19:11

> A man's wisdom gives him patience; it is to one's
> glory to overlook an offense.

There are some questions you can ask yourself to decide if you need to speak to the person.

Am I a close enough friend to the person that they will know I am speaking out of love?

Is this my problem or the other person's?

Is this issue important to the person's soul? (Will it matter in a thousand years?)

What am I doing this to help or to wound?

Am I upset because I have a similar sin that I don't wish to admit?

Can I say this with love and not in a negative way?

Do I nag about this?

God gave you grace, should I give grace?

Really marinate in this awhile before jumping the gun and rushing to announce your forgiveness. When thinking about this situation, always remember to look at the person as a soul. Think about how this will affect their soul. If it is detrimental to their soul, have a kind heart and speak to them. If it does not affect their soul forgive them in private and move on.

When we look at situations, we often overlook our part that may have contributed to the outcome. If someone abused you as a child. This is not for you. But if you treated someone with disrespect or bitterness, you might have paid a part in someone else's failures. Don't blame yourself for the other's sins; however except your own faults. For example, have you ever said something to someone without thinking and ending up doing more harm than good? Did you ever think about praying before you opened your mouth? My husband used to always tell me, "You can't say that?" My normal response was, "I just did." He did this so often that I now censor myself and when I see someone coming at me. I say a prayer for God to censor my mouth. What a difference it has made. We often forget about this. Preachers and teachers pray to get their hearts right before speaking. Why aren't we praying before conversions?

Paul told us, in Galatians. How to approach someone who sins. Instead of attacking him or her, speak to them gently. For example, "I was hurt by what you said about me to other people."

Galatians 6:1

> "Brothers and sisters, if someone is caught in a sin, you who live by the Spirit should restore that person gently. But watch yourselves, or you also may be tempted."

You also need to be that gentle with yourself. Learn from your mistakes and try to move forward. Everyone sins not just you. You made a mistake that is in the past. Move forward and try not to make that mistake again. Always remember Ephesians 4:32, "Be kind and compassionate to one another, forgiving each other, just as in Christ God forgave you."

Dig Deeper

Ask God to help you identify and work on any acid or unforgiveness in your heart.

Pray for the person whom you need to forgive. Genuinely ask for God to move in their lives and grant them peace.

List all the talents and gifts God has given the person or person's you need to forgive, including yourself.

_____

_____

_____

_____

When you see these people, think on their gifts, not their actions.

Every time you forgive do it with humility. Remember they are a soul that sins in a different way than you do.

During the upcoming week Read Ephesians 4: 31-32, every morning.

> "Let all bitterness and wrath and anger and clamor and slander be put away from you, along with all malice. Be kind to one another, tenderhearted, forgiving one another, as God in Christ forgave you."

Pray every day for forgiveness and for help to forgive.

Chapter 11- Stop Reliving it

We all have deep scars that are a result of some horrible situations or actions. I have a very vivid memory and Satan loves to remind of ways I messed up and dishonored God. When I was younger, I met a man whom I liked and started dating. Before long, we moved in together. This man talked me into moving away from my family and friends. Then He began to belittle me and berate me just a little at a time. At first, it was the way that cooked and dressed. Then it grew and he would tell me how dumb I was or say "Can't you get anything right," and his favorite thing to do, seemed to be, to make me feel horrible and incompetent. At first, I would try to speak up, and he would cut me off with "It is not the time or the place" and walk off.

At this time he stopped letting talk to my family or friends on the phone. I would be standing right there, and he would tell them I wasn't home. There were some times when he wasn't around that I would call trying to talk to my family. For my birthday my mom and Dad wanted to take me out for supper. He blew a gasket. I remember thinking what's the big deal. He pouted and yelled but finally gave in because it was my birthday. He said he was planning a surprise for me and I ruined it by wanting to see my parents. This is how he would turn everything around to be my fault. He isolated me so that his friend were our friends. I worked, and he started taking my check as soon as I got it and I had to beg for money to buy groceries.

Over time, this all elevated and the comments would be more and harsher. He would tell me, "I am the only one who will ever love you," "Why would anyone love you," and "You don't know how to do anything right." There came a point when I stopped arguing, dropped my head and I agreed. I believe now, he knew he had broken my spirit. Remember this was during the dark years when I was running from God. God was still present I just refused to go to him. After my spirit was broken, he then began to escalate even further.

The first time it became physical, He was yelling at me because the dog had gotten into the trash overnight and spread it around the house. He was screaming about it being my fault because I had not tied up the trash. I yelled back that it was his dog, and he let him inside. There was clap and horrible sting in the face, as I realized he had just slapped me. Later he apologized in a way that I just recently discovered as not being an apology at all. He said, "I'm sorry you made me so angry I had to slap you." This became my life. A cycle of him getting angry getting more and more physical and then coming back with an apology that made it all my fault. I felt isolated, worthless and unloved.

While all of this is happening I was beating up myself mentally, as much as, he was physical. I would remember how women I loved and respected would say things like, "If a man hits you once it is his fault, if he hits you twice it's your fault." It kept running through my mind that stronger Christian ladies would be able to leave. But I couldn't. I honestly believed I couldn't survive on my own. I became pregnant and we decided to get married. So I contacted my parents, and we began to make some decisions. My mom came and got me to shop for some wedding stuff, and we were in the car headed toward Dallas and my mom said, "Why are you marrying him?" I replied, "He is the only one who will ever love me." At this moment, I truly believed that with all my heart. Satan has used this man to completely and utterly break me.

It all came to a head one night we were having a particularly violent fight and ran to the bathroom and dropped to the floor. I sat there with my body pushed up against the door while he was banging and yelling on the other side. I remember thinking I can't raise a child in this. I began to pray, for probably the first time in months. At that moment, I just cried out to God and asked for forgiveness and asked for him to help me get out because I couldn't do it on my own. He eventually stopped beating on the door and left. I crawled out of the bathroom and called my family. My sister said I could come to stay with her. This is why I always say. My son saved my life. It took me loving that baby inside me enough to say that prayer and ask for help. At that point, I didn't love myself enough to leave, but the fear and love for my child made me come back to Jesus.

I told you from the beginning I would be transparent with you I had to tell you that about myself to tell you this. My son has graduated now. No one knew this, but my husband now, up until about 7 years ago when I spoke to our youth about self-esteem. In fact, when people would ask why I left I would tell them because he had cheated on me. He had cheated on me but that was months before. It was just easier to lie than to let people know how weak I really was. Then 2 years ago, I spoke at a women's conference and told my testimony. Even though for about 16 years I relived this time in my life at least once a month if not once a day. There are so many regrets, and I was so broken from this. I could hear his voice bashing insults at me. Reliving this time kept me from healing. He was still years later keeping me isolated. I was dealing with this pain alone. I had to give it to God and share with others to break that hold.

Remember James 5: 16, "Therefore confess your sins to each other and pray for each other so that you may be healed. The prayer of a righteous person is powerful and effective." My husband was the only person I told for the longest time. Together we prayed and he prayed for me alone. This helped me to stop letting this wound have such a hold on me. Before my husband came along I was fighting and it was me and God. God is strong enough to heal me; however, I let myself get in the way many times.

I decided when my child was born that I was a mom and that was it. I worked and took care of him. There was no way I was going to date until he was 18. It was going to be us against the world. I was building this wall around us to keep us safe. I was existing, but I was not living. God, however, had different plans. God lined this up just right that I ran across an awesome guy; I had gone to high school with. When my son was 5 my husband and I started talking. I was still very distant, but he wore me down and two years later my husband and I got married. He is the kindest and understanding man I know. He is a servant the way that God intends us to be. I am not proud to say it but on two different occasions, he snuck up behind me and to startle me and punched him. I cried and apologized. My husband just held me and let me cry. We had been married for at least a year before I ever spoke of what had happened with the man shared my son's DNA. My husband has become the best Dad and he has helped me raise our son to be the man he has become.

Reliving this time in my life kept me from forgiving the man, forgiving myself and living to my full potential. Do I still hear his voice? Yes, I do. But I combat it as I have explained in earlier chapters. I use scriptures and prayer. When a wound is so life changing like death or abuse or any other traumatic experiences, how do we stop reliving it? The first thing to know is you can't alone. You have to ask God for help and guidance daily. You are not going to wake up tomorrow and never think about this again. It will come back at you. And Satan will throw it at you at every turn. When things start to creep back in, you have to pray and hit that Bible.

You have to make a conscious effort to put this behind you. Here are some verses I used to help me deal with my past.

Isaiah 43:18-21

> 18"Forget the former things; do not dwell on the past. [19] See, I am doing a new thing! Now it springs up; do you not perceive it? I am making a way in the wilderness and streams in the wasteland. [20] The wild animals honor me, the jackals and the owls, because I provide water in the wilderness and streams in the wasteland, to give drink to my people, my chosen, [21] the people I formed for myself that they may proclaim my praise"

Psalm 103:8-12

> 8 The Lord is compassionate and gracious, slow to anger, abounding in love. [9] He will not always accuse, nor will he harbor his anger forever; [10] he does not treat us as our sins deserve or repay us according to our iniquities. [11] For as high as the heavens are above the earth, so great is his love for those who fear him; [12] as far as the east is from the

west, so far has he removed our transgressions
from us.

Take a minute with these verses. "Forget the former things;
do not dwell on the past. See, I am doing a new thing! Now it
springs up; do you not perceive it?" Is God doing new things in
you? Focus on those new things and tell Satan. That was who
I was, but this; this is who I am now. That happened yes. But
that does not define me. I am a child of God and that is where
my identity lays. Not in my mistakes. In the awesome forgiving
power of Jesus Christ. Who I am is not who I was or what
someone did to me.

"As far as the east is from the west, so far has he removed our
transgressions from us?" When we ask God for forgiveness, he
cast those sins as far as the east is from the west. HALLELUJAH!
This is fascinating to me because I am a bit weird and a big old
nerd. On Earth, you can travel south and because of the north
and south poles at some point, you are going to the South Pole
and start traveling north. East and west are different there are
no poles so you can take of east and continue traveling eastward
forever and unless you turn around you will never be traveling
west. That is awesome. " as far as the east is from the west. So
God has thrown your sins out and you can start anew.

I am always telling my sonthat until you take your last breath
life is not over. There is still time to ask forgiveness and forgive or
make different choices. You can start a new chapter in the book
of your life at any time. You just need to put it in God's hands
and move forward. Recognizing what situations and triggers
are causing you to relive your scars, will allow you to make
adjustments and memorize verses to hold onto in those times.
Remember you are not defined by what you did or what was
done to you. If you are saved, you are a child of God. No other
definition is needed.

Dig Deeper

Take some time right now to pray and ask God to show you how you are reliving your scars. And what are some triggers are in your life that leads to you reliving the past?

_____

_____

_____

_____

List any triggers you can think of that lead to you reliving the scars of your past.

_____

_____

_____

_____

If you are reliving scars, have you forgiven those involved? (Including yourself)

If you are struggling with a truly traumatic scar, talk to someone you trust and let them pray for and with you.

Ask God to help you avoid the triggers or to help you focus on scripture when these triggers arise.

This week take time to meditate on Psalms 103 in its entirety and take time to just praise God, every day. Thank Him for forgiveness and Praise Him for His love and generosity.

Memorize Isaiah 43: 18-19

18"Forget the former things;

do not dwell on the past.

[19] See, I am doing a new thing!

Now it springs up; do you not perceive it?

I am making a way in the wilderness

and streams in the wasteland.

Chapter 12 - Don't Waller in it

Being from the south, waller is a term we learn pretty early. For those who are not from the south to waller means to roll around in something as pigs that roll around in the mud. When things happen in our lives that causes scars, the natural reaction for most is to sit in our misfortune. As my mother would say, "Throw a pity party." As Christians wallering in our grief, anger, sadness or rage only keeps us from healing.

Through the Bible you see many people throwing a pity party from Elijah to the nation of Israel to Paul. Self-pity is not what God has saved us for. Christians should be the happiest most joyous people in the world. Let one bad thing happen to us and most of us want to throw our hands up and say "Why me God." When we should be waking up thanking God for what we have. Few of us have had to go through trials like Job. Somehow we end up turning ever problem into martyrdom.

I have known people in my past that just waller in their problems. When you see them or read their post online, it is always negative, and they have one more issue in their lives. It is such a downer. I have tried to combat everything they say with positives. But if I am not fighting real hard I catch myself sliding into their pity parties. When I was in 6th or 7th grade a teenage boy who went to our church was killed in a car crash. On Sunday shortly after he had died. I ask his mom how she was doing. She smiled at me and said, "God is good ALL the time." I was astonished that with all she was going through that was what she chose to say. She could have just as easily said, "fine" or "Okay." I have often thought back on that moment and said I want that faith.

Eight years ago, I was tested similarly. We found out that we were going to have twins and were ecstatic. I could tell something was wrong when we went to one of our sonograms and everyone began whispering. The babies had no heartbeat, and I was going to miscarry. I remembered back to the woman who had lost her son and how she praised God, through the pain. I tried so hard to focus on the positives and praise God for the blessings that we had.

As the story of the miscarriage got around the church, people starting coming out of the woodwork. They were telling me of their miscarriages or of their wife miscarriages. Many of the stories filled my heart because after these events God had blessed them with other children, or He had moved in their lives so much since then. A few, however, took me aback. I remember so clearly this one woman, talking about her miscarriage and how she became so depressed. Even though after that God has blessed her with two wonderful boys who at that time who where now adults. She was still angry and upset at God for the first. I remember thinking as she talked to me so that is why you are so unhappy and bitter.

I did not want to waller in my grief for years being mad at God for something I didn't understand. I was bound and determined not to be that woman. There was one decision to make I could be bitter or get better and that is a choice all of us have to make. Life is a battle and during wartime there are casualties. You can waller in it and let the enemy win or get back up and fight. In my bible study, I came across this verse.

Psalm 126:5-6

"5 Those who sow with tears

will reap with songs of joy.

⁶ Those who go out weeping,

carrying seed to sow,

will return with songs of joy,

carrying sheaves with them."

This is a promise I hold on to daily. "Those who sow with tears will reap with songs of joy." Those people who still work for God even when it seems impossible; will reap with songs of joy. When was the last time your heart sang a song of pure joy? "Those who go out weeping, carrying seed to sow, will return with songs of joy, carrying sheaves with them." Again those who continue the work will return with songs of joy. I clung to these verses and worked for God. I forced myself to get involved in things to teach and serve. It gave me a reason to pull myself out of my bed and get dressed to work for God. Not because that's what I was supposed to do. But because that's what my heart needed. There were many days I sowed in tears. There were moments when I let myself get down in the mulligrubs. But God gave me peace and some understanding. Yes, there is still some sadness when I think of how old they would be now. But there is also peace and happiness with what I am blessed with. The promise of songs of joy has been fulfilled in my life and my family. However, during these times of working through the pain, I also marinated in these verses.

1 Peter 1:6-7

> "In all this you greatly rejoice, though now for
> a little while you may have had to suffer grief
> in all kinds of trials. [7] These have come so that
> the proven genuineness of your faith—of greater
> worth than gold, which perishes even though
> refined by fire—may result in praise, glory and
> honor when Jesus Christ is revealed."

I kept repeating, "In all this, you greatly rejoice, though now for a little while you may have had to suffer grief in all kinds of trials." It helped me to focus on for a little while. I could see that a time would come when my grief would end. My mother- in -law is an amazing woman. She has battled stomach, uterine, brain and bone cancer and is winning the fight. After the stomach and uterine cancer, she was going to have brain surgery, and I was so worried and upset. She smiled at me and said, "It'll be fine. Either way, I win. If I beat this, I have more time to spend with ya'll here. If I die, I get to spend eternity in heaven." Three days after the surgery she was singing a special at her church. She could have easily been bitter, but she chose to be better. Don't be that bitter Christian. Life is too short to spend it at a pity party. When we waller in our situations, it is a denial that a trial is a test of faith.

James 1:2-4,

> "Consider it pure joy, my brothers and sisters,
> whenever you face trials of many kinds, [3]
> because you know that the testing of your
> faith produces perseverance. [4] Let perseverance

finish its work so that you may be mature and complete, not lacking anything."

Without any tests, we would not have a testimony. Even salvation is a test for us to accept Jesus and follow God's will. The tests we go through allow us to grow and mature as Christians. Because it is during those times when our decisions mean even more. Are we going to rely on God or try to go our way? Throwing your own pity party diminishes the power of God's grace. You are saying. "I am entitled to the quality of life that makes me happy." Even though this promise was not given in scripture. Jesus even says if you live for me the world will hate you.

John 16:33

"I have told you these things, so that in me you may have peace. In this world you will have trouble. But take heart! I have overcome the world."

Wallering in your situation is a selfish act. What you are saying to the world is that this is so bad that whatever someone is going through is not as bad as this. Really!! There are people in the world who live with true horrors. There are people in the world who bathe in the same river they poo in. The world has children who are starving or sold as sex slaves. Look at what God has blessed you with. I saw a sign once that said don't count your blessings share them. The best way for you to be slapped out of that selfish pity party of the flesh is to pour yourself into serving others that are not as blessed as you.

Philippians 2:3
"Do nothing out of selfish ambition or vain conceit. Rather, in humility value others above yourselves,"

Throwing a pity party focuses your time on complaining, whining, and discontent. When that time could be spent in prayer and Bible study asking for healing understanding and peace.

Philippians 4:6-8

> "Do not be anxious about anything, but in every situation, by prayer and petition, with thanksgiving, present your requests to God. [7] And the peace of God, which transcends all understanding, will guard your hearts and your minds in Christ Jesus.
>
> [8] Finally, brothers and sisters, whatever is true, whatever is noble, whatever is right, whatever is pure, whatever is lovely, whatever is admirable— if anything is excellent or praiseworthy—think about such things."

When wallering in your situation becomes a habit, it is nearly impossible to find joy. Your brain begins to think that the only way for me to have joy is if my situation is reversed. Joy does not come from situations but it is given by the Lord. If you are saved, God has given you joy. It is like an unopened package. All you have to do is accept it and open it.

1 Peter 1:8-9

> "Though you have not seen him, you love him; and even though you do not see him now, you believe in him and are filled with an inexpressible and glorious joy, [9] for you are receiving the end result of your faith, the salvation of your souls."

Focus on what God is doing in you and other instead of what has been done to you. When your fleshy self wants a pity party to remind it of Hebrews 12:2-3:

> "fixing our eyes on Jesus, the pioneer and perfecter of faith. For the joy set before him he endured the cross, scorning its shame, and sat down at the right hand of the throne of God. [3] Consider him who endured such opposition from sinners, so that you will not grow weary and lose heart."

Dig Deeper

Are there situations in your life that you are still wallering in? Focus on Psalm 126:5-6 and be reminded of the joy that comes out of working through the pain.

Psalm 126:5-6

> "Those who sow with tears will reap with songs of joy. ⁶Those who go out weeping, carrying seed to sow, will return with songs of joy, carrying sheaves with them."

Choose right now whether to be bitter or get better.

Every day this week look at your situation and find or think of three other people that have it worse off than you.

Is there something you can do to help them? Pray for them.

_____

_____

_____

_____

Take 10 minutes each day and think about how God has blessed you.

Do you have a place to live? (God gave you that)

_____

_____

_____

_____

Do you have a job or set retirement? (God gave you that)

_____

_____

_____

_____

Do you have food and clean water? (God gave you that)

_____

_____

_____

_____

Did you wake up this morning and breathe? (God gave you that)

_____

_____

_____

_____

Pray and ask God to help you find peace and understanding. Ask Him to open your heart and eyes to his blessings and to help you push your selfishness back.

Chapter 13 - Look at Your Scars Through God's eyes

While going through this journey with God to change my battle scars to beauty marks, I started looking at my life in a completely different manner. I hope you remember 2 Corinthians 12:9, "But he said to me, "My grace is sufficient for you, for my power is made perfect in weakness." Therefore I will boast all the more gladly about my weaknesses, so that Christ's power may rest on me." In order for me to see God's power, I had to look back at my scars through God's eyes. This was a huge turning point for me. I hope that you will be able to do the same and see God's power in your life.

My miscarriage was a hard time for our family. But it was a time when our bonds as a family grew and our faith in God. When I step out of myself and see what happened afterward, I know God's power. After my miscarriage, God gave me a love for children that I never had before. I now have a deep desire to see children learn about God's love. Since then God has allowed me to write six Vacation Bible School curriculums and be the director of Vacation Bible School at my church. The joy I receive from watching the kids have fun and learn about the Lord is immeasurable. God's work in my life made that scar beautiful.

Romans 8:28-32

"And we know that in all things God works for
the good of those who love him, who[a] have been
called according to his purpose. [29] For those God
foreknew he also predestined to be conformed
to the image of his Son, that he might be the
firstborn among many brothers and sisters. [30]
And those he predestined, he also called; those
he called, he also justified; those he justified, he
also glorified.

[31] What, then, shall we say in response to these
things? If God is for us, who can be against us?
[32] He who did not spare his own Son, but gave
him up for us all—how will he not also, along
with him, graciously give us all things?"

When I think about the pain and abuse I went through in
an abusive relationship and I think about what God has done
with that, I see the world differently. I love and appreciate my
husband so much more than I probably would have if I had
not been through that. I can identify and speak to people who
have gone through the same things. I can be a voice for those
without a voice. There have been multiple times since I left that
man that I have talked to people about how an abused person
feels because people who have never lived it do not understand.
Once I was keeping the nursery at a church and two women
were talking about a girl in an abusive relationship, and they
keep on about why she just doesn't leave. I sat there trying to
compose myself to speak and tears began to run down my
check and I said in a shaky voice, "She doesn't leave because she
can't." I went on to explain that at this point she is broken and

probably has little to no self-worth, and she can't leave because she doesn't think she can make it. This exact conversion has happened multiple times. I realize now, God didn't want me to make the bad decisions I made, but it doesn't stop Him from allowing me to open people's minds about this situation.

I can do this all day. Tell you how God has used bad things to do good when we let him. Look through the bible there are many people with worse scars than most of us. God used those things to change the world. The story of Joseph in the Old Testament was the first one to come to mind. His brothers hated him because he had a dream that they would bow to him. So they threw him into a pit and then sell him into slavery, and his boss's wife lied about him and accused him of attempted rape. He is thrown in prison. And there he interpreted dreams, and he hoped that Pharaoh's cup bearer would get him out. But he forgets about Joseph for two more years. He had about seventeen years of bad things happening. He then interprets a dream for Pharaoh and Pharaoh gives him the position of second in command and puts him in charge of all the food in Egypt. God then used him to save his family and in turn the entire nation of Israel. I am sure Joseph was scarred by the bad situations in his life but God used those things to bring him to the right place at the right times. The things he learned during his seventeen years separated from his family molded him into the man that would save them. Joseph even says it in Genesis 50:20, "You intended to harm me, but God intended it for good to accomplish what is now being done, the saving of many lives."

Job is another biblical character that my scars seem to pale in comparison to. You may remember how many truly horrific things happened to Job. He lost his house, his children, his livestock, and he had horrid health problems. Through it all, he believed in the powerful hand of God, even though Satan was wreaking havoc on his life. And in the last chapter of Job, the writer says his family and friends gathered in Job 42:11 "All his brothers and sisters and everyone who had known him before came and ate with him in his house. They comforted and consoled him over all the trouble the Lord had brought on him, and each one gave him a piece of silver and a gold ring." So from Job and the writer's point of view, God did not just bring good things out of Job's misery, but that He gave a purpose to Job's misery. James 5:11 says, "As you know, we count as blessed those who have persevered. You have heard of Job's perseverance and have seen what the Lord finally brought about. The Lord is full of compassion and mercy."

Ruth's story is another full of tragedy and sadness. Ruth was married to Naomi's son. Naomi's husband and their two sons died. Naomi took Ruth to Bethlehem. They had very little food and Ruth went out into a field and picked grain that had fallen on the ground. Boaz the owner of the field took notice of her. He was a relative of Naomi. Boaz was kind to them and gave them grain. Ruth and Boaz were married and had a son Obed who was the father of Jesse and Jesse was the father of David. God used the tragedy of Ruth and Naomi to bring them to Bethlehem and show them how God's hand could direct them through the pain.

Another example is the experience of Esther. It would be pretty devastating for a young, beautiful, Jewish girl to be forced into the harem of a pagan king. That is exactly what it was. Taken from your people and family. Esther was able to use her position with the king to help when Mordecai tells her Jews were about to be slaughtered by Haman one of the kings viceroys. She is able to use her status with the King to save her people. God did through Esther, exactly what he did for through Joseph. She came to the kingdom, through all her humiliation and defilement, to save God's people.

All of these Bible characters went through things that I am sure left scars. God was still able to use them and their scars for great things. We all have scars that we have difficulty seeing how God can use them. Especially if its sin. Nothing is impossible for God. Looking at your life through God's shows you just how useful and powerful you can be. God did not make us to be timid. He made you to be bold. Be bold about how God worked through your scars.

There is a myriad of ways that opening up about your scars and being honest about yourself and what God has done for you can help others. We can warn people of the dangers of sin we have experienced. We can talk to people who may be dealing with it issues currently that you have dealt with in the past. You could start a support group for people with the same scars. God will turn those unsightly things we believe are too ugly to show others into beauty marks. He may have already started in you.

Dig Deeper

Take time to look back at one of your scars and see it through God's eyes.

How has God changed you as a result of that scar?

_____

_____

_____

_____

What good has been the result of that scar?

_____

_____

_____

_____

    Think about how you can show others the power of God by boasting in your weakness.

    Pray and ask God to show you how He has worked in your life and ask him to show you how He sees you.

    Pray and ask God to show you how He has worked in your life and ask him to show you how He sees you.

Chapter 14 - See God's Grace

The verse that started this entire journey was 2 Corinthians 12:9, But he said to me, "My grace is sufficient for you, for my power is made perfect in weakness." Therefore, I will boast all the more gladly about my weaknesses, so that Christ's power may rest on me. Read this again My grace is sufficient for you. Grace. Grace is a word that I had heard my entire life. But it wasn't until a few years ago when I was asked to do a bible study at our church over Amazing Grace did I truly understand its meaning.

The Bible study was for a group of women from 25 to 90 and I started out with, "What is Grace?" No one could give me a definitive answer. Scriptures were referenced but a definition of what grace was not in them. You have to fully understand grace to appreciate salvation. Most people combine grace and mercy or confuse the two. Mercy is not getting a punishment you deserve. For example, if my son was to break a rule, I could have mercy on him and not ground him. Mercy is what you plead to get out of a punishment. Grace is getting something good you never deserved. No matter how hard I work and how much I give I will never deserve to go to heaven.

It today's society, people have this idea that we all deserve something for nothing. People show up to work on time, and they expect a raise. It's your job to be there on time. Try doing your job or going the extra mile before asking for a raise. It is in every part of our lives. People believing that God should bless them just because they were born. We are all sinful wretched fleshy beasts that literally deserve nothing. My son is always asking me to get him things. My answer is always, "Why should I buy you that?" He responds with, "I deserve it or I want it." I say, "What have you done to deserve it?" I could give him grace and buy the stuff. Sometimes I do, but more times than not he works for what he wants or waits till he has money.

Ephesians 2:8-9

> For it is by grace you have been saved, through faith—and this is not from yourselves, it is the gift of God— not by works, so that no one can boast.

Think about it. Because God gave us something we never deserved, we have been saved. It is not about anything we have done it is a gift from God who loves us. It is not because of anything we have done so don't act like it is. How often have you thanked God for His grace in your life? Do you ever even take the time to think about how many times he has shown you grace.

> 2 Timothy 1:9 says, "He has saved us and called us to a holy life—not because of anything we have done but because of his own purpose and grace. This grace was given us in Christ Jesus before the beginning of time."

Before God created the earth, He knew we would need to be rescued from sin. Throughout the Bible from Genesis to

Revelations, God's grace is apparent. Look at Noah, Genesis 6:8(KJV), "But Noah found grace in the eyes of the lord." At this point, the entire world was full of wicked men. Noah was not perfect, yet God gave him and his family salvation. Even though Abraham and Sarah did not fully believe God that she would have a child, God gave them a son. He showed them grace. Moses doubted that God could make him the man God told him he was. God walked with Moses and even called him a friend, knowing that Moses had once killed a man with his bare hands. That is grace. This is only a couple of examples in Genesis and Exodus. Image if we just read the bible and wrote done all the times God showed grace. That book would be as big as a large print version unabridged version of war and peace. It is so evident in the Bible. Why do we forget about it in our lives?

Working with teens, I have seen and heard some horror stories of what they have gone through. And every time my son would start to talk bad or gossip about someone I would say, "It is only by the grace of God that you are not in that situation." After spending time studying grace I really understood that statement for the first time. It is by the grace of God that we have the life we have. I don't deserve any of the amazing things God has given me. If we went on a points' system with God, I would probably live in a hole in the ground and have to eat grub worms to survive. But God has granted me grace and given me a family, a house, a car, food, love and everything I need. God gives us things not because we deserve them, but because He loves us. It is only right to thank him for that grace.

I was speaking to a friend of mine who had another friend whose baby was stillborn. My friend was distraught saying how the parents had got their life right, and they were going to church. I said we don't know God's plans, and we don't know what hardships they may have had or what Satan had in mind. She said, "Why do bad things happen to good people?" I replied, "You're asking the wrong question. When you ask the right question, I will tell you the answer." She then replied, "Why do good things happen to bad people?" I said, "Nope that isn't it." We sat in silence for about five minutes when she finally burst out with, "Okay! What's the right question?" My reply was simple, "How is it that a God who created the world, gave us life and everything good in it, who knows what we did yesterday. Who knows what we thought yesterday, knows what we didn't do that we should have yesterday allow us to wake up today and draw breath?" That is the question we should ask. We have to realize this life is not about us. We have to stop making it about us. This life is about God and spreading his kingdom. Satan is going to attack and is going to make us want to question God. But when we stop making it about us and start making life about God. We see his grace and it is that much sweeter.

God said to Paul, "My grace is sufficient for you." The original word for sufficient here is Arkeo. Arkeo means to be satisfied or suffice. It doesn't say everything is going to be sunshine and roses, but what it does say is God's grace will satisfy you. It can make you happy with what you have. Have you ever looked to see the grace in your life? Are you starting to see a bit of God's grace in you? Romans 6:23 says, "The wages of sin is death, but the gift of God is eternal life through Jesus Christ our Lord." We are all born into sin, even as little babies. Grace in this verse and in our lives is the comma. The wages of sin is death. Period. Full Stop. This is what we deserve. However; God being the forgiving loving God he is added a comma. That comma was His Grace. The story doesn't end at death. Instead of receiving what we deserve, we are given the choice of a gift. The best gift you will ever receive, it is eternal life with Jesus.

Grace says, "I know you don't deserve this, but I'm going to give it to you anyway."

Looking at my life and scars I can see how I messed up. But I also see how God's grace was with me through it all. Many times, during the dark years, I did things that could have gotten me abducted, hurt, or killed. God protected me, even when I didn't protect myself. I don't deserve to be writing this Bible study. I don't even deserve to be alive. Every moment of my life is full of God's grace.

Look at your scars and see how God allowed for good moments in sad times. See how God provided all you needed. Was there someone who helped you through or just allowed you to cry? Was there a time when money was tight but God provided? What about when all seemed lost and a way out was shown to you. If you got up this morning and took a breath, you have experienced God's grace today.

Dig Deeper

Have you been overlooking God's grace in your life?

_____

_____

_____

_____

Look back at the times when things scarred you and look for God's grace.

Right down five times in your life that God granted you grace and you have never thanked him for it.God's grace is enough to satisfy you. Make an effort this week to thank God for specific acts of grace you see Him do daily.

_____

_____

_____

_____

Read Ephesians 2:8-9, every morning this week and focus your thoughts on God.

For it is by grace you have been saved, through faith—and this is not from yourselves, it is the gift of God— not by works, so that no one can boast.

Pray and asked God to help you to focus more on Him and less on you. Ask him to help you see his hand in your life.

Chapter 15 - Ponder God's Plan

We all know God has a plan for our lives and at times it may seem like a mystery. Pondering God's plan focuses on what God wants for you. Like I said in the previous chapter, it is not about you. Pondering or thinking about God's plan for your life allows you to focus on the beauty in those scars or the God can use them for His glory. The last things Jesus said on earth we often call the great commission.

Matthew 28: 19-20

> "Therefore go and make disciples of all nations, baptizing them in the name of the Father and of the Son and of the Holy Spirit, [20] and teaching them to obey everything I have commanded you. And surely I am with you always, to the very end of the age."

When I am leaving the house or my husband and son are leaving, I will repeat important information as I leave. The last words I say are what I want them to hear the most. Think about when you are giving instructions or directions to someone. You often go back over the important bits at the end. This is exactly what Jesus was doing. I want you to remember this. Go and tell people about me and teach them how to do what they are supposed to do to have an abundant life with me. This is God's plan for all of us. Everyone has different ways of doing this. Some preach, some teach, some love and accept everyone, some sing, some cook for the hungry there are many paths, but they are based in the same plan.

In Sunday school last Sunday we went over Psalms 90: 10-12 which says, "Our days may come to seventy years, or eighty, if our strength endures; yet the best of them are but trouble and sorrow, for they quickly pass, and we fly away. [11] If only we knew the power of your anger! Your wrath is as great as the fear that is your due.[12] Teach us to number our days that we may gain a heart of wisdom."

We are limited in the amount of time we have here on earth. What exactly are we doing with that time?

If someone was to say to you, "what do you want to have accomplished by the time you turn 70?" What would you say? While you are thinking about that if a doctor told you-you had one year left to live, would you start trying to reach goals faster? We are not guaranteed any number of days. I could have a heart attack typing this chapter or you could have an accident on your way home from the bookstore. Life is fleeting, so why are we living like we have a good 30 more years?

James 4:14

> "Why, you do not even know what will happen tomorrow. What is your life? You are a mist that appears for a little while and then vanishes."

If God has put something on your heart to do, don't waste time. Because we are as a mist. God has called all saved people to do something. That is his plan for you. If you have a passion or burden for something or a group of people think about what

God wants you to do, pray about it and start working towards it. My husband and I were talking, and he said that he has been thinking about the fact that he has a perfectly functioning body and there are people out there that have to work hard just to get in a car. He said he felt like he should be doing more. We discussed what he could do, and he decided to pray and ask God to open some doors for him to do more. God's plan is always the expansion of his kingdom.

1 Peter 4:10-11

> "Each of you should use whatever gift you have received to serve others, as faithful stewards of God's grace in its various forms. [11] If anyone speaks, they should do so as one who speaks the very words of God. If anyone serves, they should do so with the strength God provides, so that in all things God may be praised through Jesus Christ. To him be the glory and the power for ever and ever. Amen."

God has given you a gift. Some of my gifts, passions, and talents were born in the sorrow or pain of my scars. Because I spent so many years running from God I have the desire to help teens and young adults avoid the same pitfalls I did. When I had a miscarriage God put in me a love for children and a desire for all of them to hear of God's love. God can create passions and desires in you from your scars. Our church has a bereavement class for widows and widowers that were born out of one lady's pain of losing her husband. God will use those scars for good if you give them to Him.

So your scars heal and you start seeing God's hand in your life, you need to see how your beauty marks and your talents can be used to further God's kingdom. The key is further God's Kingdom not your agenda. What are you doing or what can you do to help others come to God. A wonderful lady in our community opened her house for a weekly bible study for single moms. She was not a single mom she was a grandma and had a playroom with toys. She watched the kids every Thursday night as the moms sat in the front room and held a bible study. When I met this woman, it had been going on for seven years and that was six years ago. Someone mentioned to her a desire for a bible study, and she stepped up. The Bible study has grown from just single moms to women in general. God's plan is working through her because she wanted to see women grow in their knowledge of God.

On the other hand, I have known some churches that have closed their doors because they lost their way. Some of these churches had people came to church on Sunday morning to be seen or network. They had no desire to serve God or to spread God's word. As I look back these churches they had one thing in common. They had not reached out into the community. They have no outreach programs or service programs for the community and that their ministries were all designed to benefit the members. In my option, the people of these churches had lost sight of God's plan. They did not have a desire to learn or grow and lost the fire to reach out to others. I use these churches as an example, is your Christian life like this. You show up on Sunday morning dressed real nice but once the invitation is over so is your desire to reach out for God. Remember our days on earth are numbered but our soul will live forever. How concerned are you about the souls of others and how can you push yourself aside and serve God?

God gave every saved Christian a gift they are supposed to use to serve others and spread God's word. What are your gifts?

If you can't see your gifts what are you passionate about? What is our innermost desire? Can you use those things to further God's kingdom?

Dig Deeper

Ask yourself the following questions.

What Spiritual gifts do I have? (If you do not know there are several tests online to show you your gifts)

_____

_____

_____

_____

Has God given me a talent?

_____

_____

_____

Do other people say you are good at something?

_____

_____

_____

What are you passionate about?

_____

_____

_____

_____

God will use what he has put in you for His plan. Be open to ideas and suggestions from others.

Write down three talents or skills that God has given you.

_____

_____

_____

How can each of these skills to further God's Kingdom?

_____

_____

_____

_____

Spend time this week pondering how God can use you in his plan.

Pray and ask God to show you ways you can be used for his plan and live for him.

Chapter 16 - Share your Beauty Marks

I hope that throughout this book you have been able to see those scars as something beautiful. Not because of what you did or was done to you, but because of what God has done and what he is still doing. We are going to look back again at 2 Corinthians 12:9, But he said to me, "My grace is sufficient for you, for my power is made perfect in weakness." Therefore I will boast all the more gladly about my weaknesses, so that Christ's power may rest on me. Can you see how God's power is made perfect in our weaknesses? Now we have to learn to boast even more about our weakness.

Admitting that we messed up is a huge thing for Christians. For some reason, we have this idea that no one needs to know that we are human and make mistakes. This is a big problem. When we can't see you for who you are we can never truly know you. I am weird and I embrace that. I made mistakes and it was much easier to say that I am a broken person that makes bad choices. The only reason I am as together as I am is that I am held together by prayer and duck tape make of God's love and grace. In today's world with social media everybody is trying to take the best pictures with the right filters and no one sees the real you. Everyone wants the best profile picture and wants to post pictures of all the places they go to. I just want people to admit they are sinners and that God saved them through Jesus.

One of the hardest things I had to do when I was pregnant was to walk into church. I was single, pregnant, and doing my best. I was so afraid of what people were going to say that it kept me from worshiping God for months. Walking into that church knowing that everyone knew I had committed a sin was terrifying. I had let my parents down, let my preacher down, let all of my teachers down and let God down most of all. I was lucky my pastor and his wife loved on me and told me how proud they were that I had not gotten an abortion. My fears were not unfounded though many people in the church did point and whisper. Then I realized; I sinned and so did they. You could just see the effects of my sin. While they were not accepting me and not showing God's love, they were gossiping, lying, and committing sins of their own. All have sinned. I had to be reminded that I had asked for forgiveness and repented of that sin and it was OK with me and God.

When Jesus was on earth, He meets a demon-possessed man. This man did not wear clothes and lived in the tombs or graveyard. Jesus cast out the demons and they went into a herd of pigs. The pigs then ran off a cliff. After this, the man wanted to follow Jesus, but Jesus knew he could be more useful in his own town. Luke 8:38-39 says, The man from whom the demons had gone out begged to go with him, but Jesus sent him away, saying, [39] "Return home and tell how much God has done for you." So the man went away and told all over town how much Jesus had done for him." So the man went away and told all over town how much Jesus had done for him." He ran off and told everyone who knew him how Jesus had saved him. They all knew he was possessed and remembered him as living in the tombs, but he told them what God did for him. His testimony was more powerful because they knew how much he had changed.

Take the bandages off your life and let people see the real you. When we see you, we can see God's power on you. Because we can see how he has forgiven and blessed you, in spite of your wretched fleshy self. James 5:16 says, "Therefore confess your sins to each other and pray for each other so that you may be healed. The prayer of a righteous person is powerful and effective." We seem to think it okay to ask for prayer for illness but rarely do we ask for prayer for sin in our lives. I am not perfect. I am selfish and prideful and quick to anger and those are just a few. If I tell you of this you can pray for me and I rejoice in prayers because I need them.

Throughout the Bible, we read stories of people who sinned, mad bad choices and just ran from God. We learn how to deal with those types of situations because of what they went through and how God used them. What makes us any better than them that we can't say, "I am a complete mess, but God still loves me." I am so tired of people putting on masks to show people a fake person. I love you for you. God made you who you are, not who you pretend to be. What would we ever learn if all we ever heard from David was that he killed a giant, won some wars and became king? That is fine and dandy but what about his adultery, murder, and pride. He would ask forgiveness and mess up again in another way. God still loved him. Or Jonah, God told him to go to Nineveh, some stuff happened and people turned away from their sins and repented. We miss out on all the amazing things God did for Jonah and How God even provided him shelter when he pouted. This could go on for days. You think of your favorite bible story. What if all that was in that story was how we let people see us? The Glory of God would be missing. This is what we are missing in our lives. The power of God. Every person has a testimony it can be as powerful or as weak as you want. If you show that wretched part of you and explain how God changed that then that is when it becomes powerful.

Psalm 71:15-16

> "My mouth will tell of your righteous deeds, of your saving acts all day long— though I know not how to relate them all. [16] I will come and proclaim your mighty acts, Sovereign Lord; I will proclaim your righteous deeds, yours alone."

Don't hide behind your profile picture anymore. Tell of what God has done for you. It's okay. This entire book is about battle scars. It's about life being a battle and armoring up. How to heal from scars. We sing about being in the Lord's army and about being a conqueror and an overcomer. But we are too scared to step up and show how God has moved in our lives. A wonderful friend of mine Jill Brandon has written this fabulous song called "Warrior." The song starts with, "I am a warrior, a fighter, an overcomer nothing's stopping me. I am a warrior I am stronger, I am a warrior, a fighter, an overcomer nothing's stopping me, and I am not giving up." We want to seem like a strong warrior woman of God. Where is our fighting spirit? Where is our faith? If God has helped you overcome something, claim it. Shout out what God has done for you. Don't hide behind a facade. Show the world how God loves everyone even the broken, bruised and wounded. Do you want to see God's rest on you? Then stand up and tell somebody what His power has done for you.

Dig Deeper

In the next chapter, you will create your testimony. Meditate on Psalm 71:15-16

> "My mouth will tell of your righteous deeds, of your saving acts all day long— though I know not how to relate them all. [16] I will come and proclaim your mighty acts, Sovereign Lord; I will proclaim your righteous deeds, yours alone."

Reread your favorite Bible story and take a mental note of the sin, bad choices, weakness and faults of the characters.

List how God's knowing the people's weaknesses showed God's power.

_____

_____

_____

_____

List some key times in your life when God has shown you a glimpse of his power.

_____

_____

If you have a scar that you have never told anyone about, find someone you trust and tell them.

Every morning as you pray, ask God to give you opportunities to talk about what he has done for you.

Pray and ask God to give you boldness and put your pride and selfishness aside and help you to be honest about who you are.

Chapter 17 - Testify

All through the Bible, we are told to tell others what God has done for us. And when you talk to people about their testimony they normally tell you about when they got saved and how God changed their lives then. That is great! But what has happened since then? God has saved my soul, and I am eternally grateful. He has also shown his power in awesome ways since then. Remember 2 Corinthians 12:9, "But he said to me, "My grace is sufficient for you, for my power is made perfect in weakness." Therefore I will boast all the more gladly about my weaknesses, so that Christ's power may rest on me." Boast means to tell people about something. Your story or your testimony is everything God has done for you. It starts at birth leads to salvation and is continuing throughout your life.

I am not saying to sit down write out an autobiography all about you. What I am saying is to not limit yourself to the moment of salvation. 1 Peter 3:14-16 says, "But even if you should suffer for what is right, you are blessed. "Do not fear their threats; do not be frightened." [15] But in your hearts revere Christ as Lord. Always be prepared to give an answer to everyone who asks you to give the reason for the hope that you have. But do this with gentleness and respect, [16] keeping a clear conscience, so that those who speak maliciously against your good behavior in Christ may be ashamed of their slander."

Always be prepared to give an answer to anyone who asks you to give the reason of hope you have. Be ready to speak to anyone and give them hope. You may not have gone through the same trail or tragedy, but you have had a few. Be ready to give hope by showing why you have hope. The hope that we have through Jesus Christ should be our whole story. It should be what everything in our lives points back to.

The goal of creating your testimony is to give glory to God. No matter how ordinary or trivial you think your problems or trials were; they are yours. The story is about who God is. God's hand and glory can be seen in some places we never seem to look. For example; has God helped you buy a car or house? Or maybe groceries when times were tough? Of course, He did! Everything beautiful, good and special in our lives came from God. This is how we tell other of Christ through everything God has done for us. Your testimony is your eyewitness account of how God rescued you from sin and death through Christ, how He held you in His arms when you wept, and how His grace healed you. It is everything He has done for you.

When we tell others what God has done for us, we help them to get a window into what God is like and all that he has done and will do. When you start to gather your thoughts together, you need to keep this in mind. It is not about me it's about God. When I testify, I make sure that I explain that Missy has never done anything good or noteworthy that God didn't do for her or give her. When she was running from God and doing what Missy wanted, she messed things up on a nuclear level. There is nothing good inside Missy that God didn't put there. My testimony is not how I mess up or what happened to me or the loss I experienced, but it is how God stepped in and fixed it or fixed me or comforted me or forgave me or blessed me. Your testimony should be a Godie, not a selfie.

When we start talking to people about our testimony, we can get distracted. "Oh, something shiny" or "Squirrel." This why creating your testimony is so valuable. It allows you to really focus on it. And look at it objectively. You can make sure you have seen exactly how God worked in you. Do memorize what you have written but know it well enough to recall what the message was about.

You are about to take some notes. Go get a pen and paper and get ready. When you answer these questions make sure that you have focused on God and not on yourself. There are some things you should avoid when pulling all this together. Try not to be formal or fake. Write the way you speak. If you speak using a bit of slang, write it. Be yourself. Try not to be overly negative or positive. Be honest. Do your best to avoid naming negative people, churches, denominations, or organizations. Not everyone in an organization is the same and there are many people that may have the same names as well as the fact that since that moment God may have changed that person or people, and they may not be anything like they were.

Remember your testimony should be your love letter to God. Testify to what you know. That is all God asked you to do.

Dig Deeper

STOP!! Pray for God's hand to guide you through the process.

Think about the moment Jesus saved you and became the lord of your life.

What was life like before?

_____

_____

_____

_____

What events led up to your salvation? (How the Holy Spirit convicted you?)

_____

_____

_____

_____

Describe in detail the moment you prayed that prayer and was saved.

_____

_____

_____

_____

How did you feel afterward?

_____

_____

_____

_____

How were you changed?

_____

_____

_____

_____

Make a list of your scars.

_____

_____

_____

_____

How these scars have influenced you or what impact they had on your life?

_____

_____

_____

_____

How did God change you or the situation that caused scars?

_____

_____

_____

_____

How have you changed or grown, with God's help, to be okay with your scars?

_____

_____

_____

_____

List ways that God's Grace has blessed you when you didn't deserve it.

_____

_____

_____

_____

How can what you experienced or learned help other people?

_____

_____

_____

_____

Walk away from the list and have some quiet time with God. Ask again for guidance and strength. Think about your listener. Avoid using overly-religious terms (christianese). My husband and I taught a new believers class at our old church. One thing we discovered quite quickly was many Christians have no idea what some religious words mean. We created a list of over 40 words most new believers had no idea what they were. The list contained words like; sanctification, omnipotent, grace, transfiguration, ordinance and deacon. Never assume that they know these words or bible stories you may have grown up on. Keep it to the point. If you are just talking to people in public or conversation, aim to tell your story in three to five minutes. If you have a set time limit, for example, you are speaking to a church group and you have 30 minutes use the time given. Don't just stand up give your 3-minute spill and sit down.

Practice telling your testimony with loved ones.

The first time I gave my testimony to after the dark years; I would talk freely with my husband and practice with him and on my own to be able to do it in front of a crowd. Remember Peter tells us to be ready. Practice is getting ready.

Read what you have written. This is God's story through you. It's not over. It will not ever be completed until you draw your last breath or Jesus Christ comes back to get us. This is a snippet of what God has done for you and can do for others. Do you see it? Doesn't it fill your heart with joy? Doesn't it make you so excited you might just fall down crying, astonished at the amazing love of God? It should you should be reminded of everything God has done for you and you should want to go shout it from the rooftop. If you need to, and I did, tell a spouse, call a family member or friend or just tell the lady in front of you in line at the Dollar Tree. The first time you blurt out how God loved you and how you messed up, and He still forgave you and loved you the same, you realize you didn't die, no one stoned you, and you didn't lose respect. You gained peace and you just stand there in awe of all God has done for you.

Practice this all week and tell people close to you.

Ask Sunday school teachers or small groups leaders if you can come to share your testimony.

Do not be afraid, God is with you.

Pray for strength and boldness and tell God's story.

Chapter 18 - Continue the Healing

I hope that you have learned through this book that you are a warrior with scars. That you can heal with God's help and see your scars as beautiful. Look back at the verse we started with 2 Corinthians 12:9 "But he said to me, "My grace is sufficient for you, for my power is made perfect in weakness." Therefore I will boast all the more gladly about my weaknesses, so that Christ's power may rest on me." Does it ring more true to you now? Can you see the beauty in your life?

As you fight life's battles with Satan you will be scarred. It is inevitable. However If you are fighting with God on your side the war has already been won, by Jesus Christ. Satan may wound you or knock you down, but that is all. It is for a little while. Rely on God for strength, knowledge and direction. He will never steer you down the wrong path.

Remember

1 Peter 4: 12-19

> "Dear friends, do not be surprised at the fiery ordeal that has come on you to test you, as though something strange were happening to you. But rejoice inasmuch as you participate in the sufferings of Christ, so that you may be

overjoyed when his glory is revealed. If you are insulted because of the name of Christ, you are blessed, for the Spirit of glory and of God rests on you. If you suffer, it should not be as a murderer or thief or any other kind of criminal, or even as a meddler. However, if you suffer as a Christian, do not be ashamed, but praise God that you bear that name. For it is time for judgment to begin with God's household; and if it begins with us, what will the outcome be for those who do not obey the gospel of God? And,

"If it is hard for the righteous to be saved,

What will become of the ungodly and the sinner?"

So then, those who suffer according to God's will should commit themselves to their faithful Creator and continue to do good."

Hold these scriptures close to your heart. Know that whatever trails or temptations come your way, are not the end for us. If we suffer as a Christian, we should shout praises because we have Christ in us.

1 Peter 5: 6-11

"Humble yourselves, therefore, under God's mighty hand, that he may lift you up in due time. [7] Cast all your anxiety on him because he cares for you.

⁸ Be alert and of sober mind. Your enemy the devil prowls around like a roaring lion looking for someone to devour. ⁹ Resist him, standing firm in the faith, because you know that the family of believers throughout the world is undergoing the same kind of sufferings.

¹⁰ And the God of all grace, who called you to his eternal glory in Christ, after you have suffered a little while, will himself restore you and make you strong, firm and steadfast. ¹¹ To him be the power for ever and ever. Amen."

Remember that a battle scar is a mark or wound endured in battle. A beauty mark is a mark that is seen to enhance beauty. The major difference is that one is evidence of a wound. But a scar can be a beauty mark once it heals. The devil is still prowling and looking for those he can devour. Do not let him think he has beaten you. Stand up and fight, wounded or not our battle isn't over until God calls us home.

Ecclesiastes 3:11

"He has made everything beautiful in its time. He has also set eternity in the human heart; yet no one can fathom what God has done from beginning to end."

I was willing to show you my scars, so that you may gain the strength to show yours. God has made me beautiful because of what he has done in me and through me. Even after you have healed from your present scars, more scars may and probably are going to come your way. Remember all you have learned and never stop letting God heal you.

The next time you are wounded, do not wait or let it fester for month or years. Take it to the great physician in prayer. Once you have gone to the doctor, you get prescription. Keep that quiet time and Bible study going. Don't let your armor of God get rusty and dull. Continue daily maintaince to protect and defend you. Your mind should always be set on what God is telling you so that you can grow as a Christian. Follow God's word and do what you are supposed to and stop being nasty. Be an encourager and lift up others. Sharing God's Joy.

As easy as Satan makes it to wallar in your self- pity chose to praise God through the pain. Stay on God's course and know that trails create endurance and perseverance, so that we can be singing God's praises when we are called home. Boast in our weaknesses, not boasting in the sin, but showing God's power through our weak times. Boast of what God has done for you. Tell the story of God through you.

Do not ever stop allowing God to work on you and through you. Let Him help you find peace and wisdom as he heals you. In Chapter 2 you saw some of my scars. The majority of those God has completely healed. The others may still hurt but I have found peace. I am not happy or content with the sins I committed and still commit, but I have learned to forgive myself and to accept God's forgiveness. And I do my best to repent and turn away from those sins and not do them again. I still slip up, I still sin. But God's Grace is sufficient for me.

I am a wretched fleshy mess whom God created and loves and so are you.

One woman in the Armor of God standing against Satan saying, "My God is the almighty God and He lives in me." Is bad for Satan. A group of warrior women in the Armor of God Standing against Satan sharing and praying and lifting each other up! That is dangerous and those women with God leading them can change the world.

Dig Deeper

Look back at the exercises in Chapter 1 and Chapter 2. Look at your list of scars

How has God changed your scars since then?

_____

_____

_____

_____

How has God changed you?

_____

_____

_____

_____

Pray to God to continue the change in you continuously throughout your life.

Go tell someone how God has healed or is healing your scars.

Printed in the United States
By Bookmasters